A
JEWISH
PHYSICIAN'S
HARVEST

Dr. Harry A. Savitz

A
JEWISH
PHYSICIAN'S
HARVEST

By

HARRY A. SAVITZ, M.D.

HEBREW COLLEGE PRESS
BROOKLINE, MASSACHUSETTS

KTAV PUBLISHING HOUSE, INC.
NEW YORK
1979

Library of Congress Cataloging in Publication Data

Savitz, Harry A
  A Jewish physician's harvest.

  Includes bibliographical references and index.
  1. Physicians, Jewish—Biography—Addresses, essays,
lectures. 2. Geriatrics—Addresses, essays, lectures,
3. Medicine—Addresses, essays, lectures. I. Title.
R694.S28   610'.92'2   [B]   78-3123
ISBN 0-87068-686-0

MANUFACTURED IN THE UNITED STATES OF AMERICA

This book is dedicated to our grandchildren with love: Rachel, David, Deborah, Evan and Jonathan Teplow; Jordan, Danny, Jonathan and Michael Finegold.

ROBERT LOUIS STEVENSON
PRAYER

When the day returns, call us up with morning faces and with merry hearts, eager to labor; happiness if happiness be our portion, and if the day be marked for sorrow, strong to endure.

כְּבֹא הַיּוֹם עוֹרְרֵנוּ נָא בְּפָנִים מְאִירוֹת וּבְלֵב שָׂמֵחַ, נִלְהָב וְלָהוּט לַעֲבוֹדָה, מְאֻשָּׁר אִם אֹשֶׁר הוּא חֶלְקֵנוּ וְאִם חַס וְחָלִילָה מַר הוּא גוֹרָלֵנוּ חַזְּקֵנוּ וְאַמְּצֵנוּ לְנָשֹׁא.

Hebrew Translation
by
Dr. Harry A. Savitz

Contents

ix

Foreword

Throughout the long and inspiring history of the Jewish people, there have been many examples of joining together the medical practitioner and the model Jewish person. The healer of man and the servant of God have frequently been seen as one and the same; Aaron, the high priest; Maimonides and Judah Ha-levi represent this type of individual.

Dr. Harry A. Savitz, whom I have come to know intimately over the years, has been in the mainstream of this elect tradition. A past president and honorary trustee of Hebrew College, a dedicated Jewish scholar, a warm human being, and a distinguished physician, he has gained not only the admiration of his medical peers, but of grateful colleagues in community work and in Hebraic scholarship.

Compassionate and warm to his patients, Harry A. Savitz was never just a physician. He would go out of his way to "drop in" unexpectedly at the home of a patient to check his progress; discussions of Jewish ethics, the Bible and Jewish life were invariably co-mingled with medical assessments. As President of Hebrew College, he brought an intimate understanding of Jewish culture to Board deliberations.

Harry A. Savitz has been a remarkable teacher. He has taught us in the numerous articles and scholarly publications, through his earlier volume *Profiles of Erudite Jewish Physicians and Scholars.* Above all, he teaches most effectively by the example of his own life—a life of rare meaning and content and commitment. A life that has strength and beauty worthy of emulating.

I regard it as a signal honor to be able to append these words of appreciation and introduction to a delightfully informative and inspiring volume by a remarkable human being: *A Jewish Physician's Harvest* by Dr. Harry A. Savitz.

Eli Grad
President, Hebrew College

Preface

This volume by Dr. Harry A. Savitz *A Jewish Physician's Harvest,*
like the earlier essays in his *Profiles of Erudite Jewish Physicians
and Scholars,* shows to a remarkable degree Dr. Savitz's profound
scholarship in medicine and Judaica, and his deep learning in a
wide range of Jewish studies from the Bible and Talmud to the
current writings in Israel and in this country.

There is much wit and humor in these pages; and there are
profound analyses of the characters of the writers and the
individuals who surround the central characters. Dr. Savitz also
has the capacity to sharpen his attack on those who try to "pass"
and to hide their Jewishness. This first became apparent many
decades ago in his essay "Spiritual Rickets," a masterpiece in
which the basic themes came from medicine, psychology and
Jewish culture, with a panoramic sweep of all of life to show
that those with "spiritual rickets" acquire the disease from their
efforts to hide their Jewishness and that spiritual rickets are akin
to physical rickets.

Dr. Savitz is more than writer and scholar, physician and student of Judaism; he is a thinker and philosopher. What he
learned from his cousin and close friend, Dr. Harry A. Wolfson,
permeates the essays in this volume. He is a teacher known to
many of his former students whom he taught in Hebrew
Schools while he was a student in the Boston Public Schools
system and during his four years at Harvard College and his
four years of Harvard Medical School. One had only to listen
to his presiding at meetings of the Boston Hebrew College or the
New Century Club, or to hear him lecture his medical staff

at the Hebrew Rehabilitation Center For the Aged, to recognize his profound knowledge of his subjects, his superb capacity to teach, his brilliant analyses, his articulate development and his charm and rich style which permitted him to give beautifully rounded talks, making complicated topics sound clear, concise and complete.

Some thirteen years ago, Dr. Savitz was the first recipient of the annual Maimonides Award "for outstanding contributions in the fields of Medicine and Judaica." This was a well-deserved award; all the institutions involved with their doctors in all their specialties, and Jewish scholars from various fields participated in the selection process; this tells as much of Dr. Savitz as any lengthy writing could possibly accomplish.

This is a book to read and enjoy. It will open eyes into fields that some of us now know and others of us never knew adequately. This is a noble feat which deserves our profound gratitude.

Lewis H. Weinstein

PART I

Biographical and Historical Studies

The Role of the Jewish Physician in the Progress of His People

The story of the Jewish physician is as long as the history of his people. In this lengthy narrative, he occupied a prominent part and played an important role. One reason for this is that the physician, from time immemorial, was held in high esteem by the Jews. Though not deified, yet he was placed on a pedestal and people looked up to him. In ancient times, the wise Ben Sira sang:

Honor a physician according to thy need of him with the honors due
   unto him:
For verily the Lord hath created him.
For from the Most High cometh healing;
And from the King he shall receive a gift.
The skill of the physician shall lift up his head;
And in the sight of great men he shall be admired.
The Lord created medicines out of the earth;
And a prudent man will have no disgust at them.   (Ecclesiasticus
   38:1–4)

This feeling of admiration for the physician has been continued up to the present time. In a much more prosaic and

Read before the Greater Boston Medical Society, October 6, 1936. First published in
Annals of Medical History, 1938.

3

vulgarized manner, it is portrayed by the *shadchen,* or match-maker, in the matrimonial market, to whom M.D. still means "More Desirable." The Jewish physician of the past appreciated this esteem and endeavored to deserve it. He not only delved into the mysteries of the healing art and science, and tried to advance it, but at the same time participated in all the great movements of his people. He not only did not shirk his duties to his people, but he even endeavored to lead and guide them.

In the formation of the Talmud, that great spiritual fortress which preserved Jews and Judaism for nearly two thousand years, a number of physicians took part. Physicians were consulted whenever medical knowledge was to be applied to legal, ritual, and ecclesiastical ordinances of Judaism, and physicians participated in a great many dicussions, adding much to the pattern of this gigantic encyclopedia. Very few physicians are mentioned by name in the Talmud, nor is there a special section dedicated to medicine. But in a perusal of its numerous pages we come across a number of physicians. One who is frequently mentioned is Theudas or Theodoros. The name of another physician, Bar Girnte, occurs in connection with his traveling in a sedan chair to visit his patients on the Sabbath owing to his advanced age. Other physicians mentioned in the Talmud as examples of genuine Jewish piety and benevolence, are Benjamin and Abba the surgeon. Although the latter was dependent upon his earnings, he was so unselfish and considerate that in order to avoid embarrassing the poor among his patients, he would never accept pay directly from anyone, but instead had attached a box to the wall in which each might place what he pleased.

Yet another talmudic physician was Samuel Yarḥina'ah (180–257 C.E.) or Mar Samuel, director of the Academy of Nehardea, who was not only a great teacher of the law but also an excellent physician, a research worker, and a great observer. He spent eighteen months with a shepherd to study eye diseases of animals. He was especially skilled in the treatment of diseases of the eye. He discovered an eye salve which came to be known as the "*killurin* of Mar Samuel." He traced many diseases to a lack of cleanliness. He made the statement that after venesection he fed his patients a meal made of spleen (*Shabbat* 129a). As a man Mar

Samuel was distinguished for his modesty, gentleness, and unselfishness, being always ready to subordinate his own interests to those of the community. He said once, "A man may never exclude himself from the community, but must seek his welfare in that of society."*

From the close of the Talmud all through the so-called Middle Ages, the thread of Jewish history was consistently being woven. There were great men in every generation who left monumental literary works. A great number of these scholars were physicians. Not only did these physicians carry on the healing art and science during the so-called Dark Ages, but in many instances it was they who advanced Jewish culture and learning in its various branches. Maimonides, whose eight hundredth anniversary was celebrated in 1935, was by no means the only star in the Jewish firmament. In the tenth century we find the famous Isaac Israeli (845–940) in North Africa. He was the author of several medical works, the best known of which is his book on fever. He also wrote a commentary on the *Sefer Yeẓirah* (Book of Creation). Graetz, the historian, says of him: "His example made a place in Rabbinic studies for the scientific method that shaped the activity of the succeeding generations."

A disciple of Israeli was Dunash ibn Tamin, a famous physician and favorite of the court, accomplished in all the known sciences, who composed an astronomical work on the Jewish calendar.

In southern Italy during the same period lived Shabbetai Donnolo (913–70), who also wrote a commentary on the Book of Creation. He was also the author of a Hebrew book on materia medica.

The contemporary of Donnolo in Spain was a Jewish physician, linguist, and statesman who was one of those who made the protection and furthering of Judaism the task of his life. I refer to the eminent physician Ḥasdai ibn Shaprut (915–70). In spite of his high position and great wealth, he felt a call to be active in the cause of his religion and race. As one historian says:

He was, to some extent, the legal and political head of the Jewish community of Cordova. He gathered around himself a band of

*See below, p. 37, for a biographical study of Mar Samuel.

talented philosophers and poets who immortalized him in their works and in their poems. More than any man he gave impetus to the unfolding of the golden period of the Judaeo-Spanish culture.[1]

The zenith of Spanish-Jewish culture was attained with two immortal physicians, Judah Halevi and Maimonides. We shall say little of the latter as our ears still echo with the orations delivered throughout the civilized world in 1935 on the eight hundredth anniversary of his birth. Judah Halevi was born in old Castile in 1086. He passed his years as a practicing physician in the city of Toledo. The historian Graetz thus eulogizes him:

In the annals of mankind his name deserves a separate page with a golden border. To describe him worthily, history would need to borrow from poetry her most glowing colors and her sweetest tones. Jehuda Halevi was one of the chosen, to whom the expression, "an image of God," may be applied without exaggeration. He was a perfect poet, a perfect thinker, a worthy son of Judaism, which, through his poetry and thought, was ennobled and idealized.

The physician Halevi was the author of a work, the *Kuzari,* which is considered one of the classics of Jewish philosophical literature. The treatise is a series of five dialogues, and is romantically framed in the medieval story of the King of the Khazars, the royal convert to Judaism. Judah Halevi takes the poet's view of Judaism and the Jews. If Maimonides' writings represent the intellect and mind of Judaism, so Halevi represents its heart and emotional side. Halevi's "Songs to Zion" are his most beautiful works, symbolizing the deepest of his emotions. One of them is chanted today in Jewish congregations all over the world, on the ninth of Av. It is an "Ode to Zion":

> Zion! wilt thou not ask if peace be with thy captives
> That seek the peace—that are the remnants of thy flocks?[2]

The following letter, which he wrote from Toledo, Spain, to a friend, more than eight hundred years ago, could be read today apropos of what is now going on in Spain:*

*Dr. Savitz is referring to the Spanish Civil War, which was well into its third year at the time that he wrote this essay (ed.).

I occupy myself in the hours which belong neither to the day nor to the night, with the vanity of medical science, although I am unable to heal. The city in which I dwell is large, the inhabitants are giants, but they are cruel rulers. Wherewith could I conciliate them better than by spending my days in curing their illness. I physic Babel but it continues infirm. I cry to God that He may quickly send deliverance unto me, and give me freedom, to enjoy rest, that I may repair to some place of living knowledge, to the fountain of wisdom.

One of the great cultural contributions of the Jews in the Middle Ages was the work of the Jewish translators. Due to the work of these scholars, Hebrew became a vehicle of expression for philosophic and scientific ideas. It also brought the learning of the Orient and the Occident together. Here again we find the Jewish physician playing an important role. This task of translation was first undertaken by Judah ibn Tibbon (1120–90), who emigrated to Provence from Spain. He translated Halevi's work. His son Samuel completed the works of the Jewish philosophers by rendering into Hebrew the *Guide to the Perplexed* of Maimonides. The translator par excellence was Moses ben Samuel ibn Tibbon, the grandson. The number of works he translated into Hebrew amounts to more than a score. Here are three generations of physicians who were engaged in this noble task. Jacob ben Abba Mari Anatoli (1200–1250), son-in-law of Samuel ibn Tibbon, upheld the family tradition and rendered many works into Hebrew. Anatoli was later employed by Frederick II of Naples to translate Arabic works into Latin.

Of the other leading translators, the most outstanding was the physician Kalonymus ben Kalonymus (1287–1337). The number of books he translated into Hebrew is considerable. Nathan ha-Me'ati of Rome translated the *Canon* of Avicenna into Hebrew (1279). Nathan ha-Me'ati also translated the *Liber ad Almansorem* of Rhazes, a unique fifteenth-century manuscript of which is in the Solomon M. Hyams Collection in the Boston Medical Library. The *Canon* of Avicenna was the most important medical text in this period.[3] There were many other physician-translators who participated in this spread of knowledge. In this way Hebrew became the key to many of the world's classics.

The outstanding scholar at the end of the thirteenth and the beginning of the fourteenth century was Levi ben Gershom

(Ralbag), also known as Gersonides (1288–1340), a renowned physician who practiced medicine in Avignon and distinguished himself in that science. He mastered practically all of the known sciences of his time, including mathematics, astronomy, and philosophy. His works on astronomy were translated into Latin, and he is known to the Gentile scholarly world as Leo Hebraeus. But to the Jewish world he is known as a commentator and philosopher. He wrote a commentary on the Pentateuch, the Prophets, Job, and the Proverbs. In these commentaries, symbolism, allegory, and philosophy were interwoven. These writings were greatly cherished by the intellectuals of subsequent generations and were well preserved. The summaries of these commentaries where the ethical teachings of the Bible are enhanced were held in such esteem that scholars of succeeding generations reprinted them separately.[4]

The most interesting figure at this time among the Jews of Italy was the physician, scholar, and satirical poet Immanuel ben Solomon of Rome (1265–1330). He was deeply versed in the Talmud and in Jewish philosophy, and mastered Hebrew, Latin, and Italian. He occupied an important position in the Jewish community in Rome and was also respected by the Gentiles, especially by the literati of the age. He was a friend and adviser of Dante, and wrote an elegy on him in Italian after Dante's death. He wrote commentaries on the Bible, a grammar of the Hebrew language, and other books, but his fame rests on his collection of poems. The outstanding characteristics of his poems are, according to Meyer Waxman, his exceptional linguistic ability and dexterous workmanship, his keen humor and biting satire, and his love of life and optimistic spirit.[5]

The following is an example of one of his satiric stanzas:

> Of what good can Paradise be
> When the company there is so boring
> Old, homely hags always snoring,
> I'd rather my Paradise sell.

On the other hand, some of his other poems reveal that he was a God-fearing man.

Immanuel also patterned after Dante a vision entitled *Ha-*

Tofet ve-ha-Eden (Hell and Paradise). As the historian Graetz puts it:

Whereas Dante's was "A Divine Comedy," his was a human comedy. Immanuel's description is free from dogmatism, and is true to human nature, and his point of view is also more human and tolerant than is the one expressed by Dante, who excludes all non-Christians as such from eternal felicity. Immanuel, entering Paradise, sees a troop of the blessed, whom he does not recognize and asks their leader who they are. "These are," answers the latter, "righteous and moral brethren, who attained the height of wisdom, and recognized the only God as the Creator of the World and the bestower of grace." Immanuel too attained for himself a place among the immortals.

But, of course, no race or profession has a monopoly on saints. There are Jews in every walk of life in every generation who crash the gates of the Gentiles and, having entered, endeavor to outdo them. In their great zeal and enthusiasm, they inflict much insult and injury to their former brethren. Of course, this is all done with a selfish motive to strengthen their own position. A classic example of this was the physician Joshua Lorki of Lorca in Spain. On his baptism he assumed the name of Gerónimo de Santa Fé, and he became physician-in-ordinary to Pope Benedict XIII. He tried to convert his brethren by every possible means. He finally urged the pope to summon the learned Jews to a religious disputation. The disputation, held in the city of Tortosa in 1413–14, lasted for sixty-nine sittings and extended over a period of more than a year. Santa Fé finally fabricated some deadly charges against the Talmud, and the enemies of the Jews accepted them without further inquiry. For this act, Santa Fé is remembered by the well-earned Hebrew sobriquet of *Megaddef* (the Calumniator).

But a character of Santa Fé's type is really an exception to the rule, and in a number of disputations it was a physician who defended the Jewish cause. As a matter of fact, one of the chief members of the committee of twenty who presented the Jewish case at this very disputation in Tortosa was the philosopher Joseph Albo, who had also been trained as a physician.

This was also true in other disputations. In 1263 another

physician and scholar, Naḥmanides, defended Judaism against another baptized Jew, Pablo Christiani. Not only did the Jewish physicians excel during these disputations and show themselves to be experts in comparative religion, but they also excelled in comparative literature. The first Jew to compare the language of the prophets and psalmists with Cicero was the physician Messer Leon, or as he is known by his Hebrew name, Judah ben Jehiel of Naples (1450–90). He was thoroughly versed in Hebrew literature and a finished Latin scholar. He wrote a Hebrew rhetoric (*Nofet Ẓufim*) in which he laid down the laws upon which the grace, force, and eloquence of style depend, and he proved that the same laws underlie the sacred literature.

In the next century we find the celebrated physician David De' Pomis (1525–93), who together with medical knowledge showed a familiarity with Hebrew and classical literature. He wrote both Hebrew and Latin with elegance. De' Pomis wrote an important literary dictionary of the Talmud in three languages. He also wrote a Latin work entitled *De Medico Hebraeo* (The Hebrew Physician). In this work he enumerated the various Hebrew physicians who had attended princes of the Christian church, cardinals and popes, and restored them to health.

There were a number of other Jewish physicians who excelled as grammarians and lexicographers.

With the invention of printing in the fifteenth century, it was a Jewish physician who became celebrated as one of the earliest printers of Hebrew books in Europe. I refer to Dr. Abraham ben Solomon Conat, who flourished at Mantua in the second half of the fifteenth century. In addition to his medical training, he must have also been a profound Hebrew scholar, for he obtained the title *ḥaver*, or associate of a rabbi, for his learning. He and his wife, Estellina, learned the art of printing. In 1475 he established a printing office at Mantua from which were produced the third to the tenth of the Hebrew incunabula, as recorded by De Rossi.

Dr. Conat displayed excellent taste in the choice of the works he selected for printing. Two of the publications are the works of physicians, the *Beḥinat Olam* (Examination of the World) of Jedaiah Bedersi (1280–1340), and the commentary on the Pentateuch of Levi ben Gershom (Gersonides), a copy of which is in the Hyams Collection.[6]

Dr. Conat was proud of his work; his name in the colophons was accompanied by the words "who writes with many pens, without the help of miracles, for the spread of the Torah in Israel." He was especially delighted that he could produce two thousand pages a day. The shape of his type was such that his editions are often taken for manuscripts.

A similar service was rendered to the Jewish people by a physician in a later century in Holland. Jewish refugees began to pour into Amsterdam and the Jewish community began to flourish. But no Jewish community is complete without books, and the production of books is impossible without printing. So we find Manasseh Ben Israel, "a divine and doctor of Physicke," as he called himself, establishing the first Hebrew printing press in Amsterdam. He was aided by a friend, the physician and litterateur Ephraim Bueno. A printing press was set up in Manasseh's own house. According to one modern historian, Cecil Roth, "This enterprise of Manasseh's was the small beginning of what became a great industry in Amsterdam. At the close of the seventeenth and throughout the eighteenth century, that city was the center of Hebrew printing for the whole world."[7]

Manasseh, like Conat, was proud of his work. He allowed nothing to appear until he had himself corrected and passed the proofs. In the introduction of a Bible in the author's collection, published by his press in 1635 (one year before the founding of Harvard College), Manasseh writes, "If my memory does not fail me, I have corrected more than three hundred mistakes. . . . With all my might and with profound love I endeavored to inspect every word, letter, and punctuation mark, etc."[8] As his distinctive printer's mark, he adopted the figure of a pilgrim with staff and bundle, and the motto *Peregranando quaerimus* ("By our wanderings we seek"), an accurate characterization of his own restless, inquiring nature.

With the rise of national consciousness in the nineteenth century and the development of the Zionist movement, we again find Jewish physicians taking a leading role. With the same skill with which they excelled in the individual struggle for existence, they exerted their energies in the eternal fight for the survival of their people and nation. It was Dr. Leon Pinsker (1821–91), long before the immortal Theodor Herzl appeared in the Jewish arena, who enunciated the message of political Zionism, in a pamphlet entitled *Autoemancipation,* which he published in German in 1881, under the nom de plume, "Ein Russischer Jude." Like a skillful, able physician, he observed the signs and symptoms of the disease of anti-Semitism, explained its cause, and prescribed remedies for it. Dr. Pinsker discovered that the cause of "our being hated and despised more than other human beings lies deep in human psychology." He wrote:

We cannot know whether that great day will ever arrive when all mankind will live in brotherhood and concord, and national barriers will no longer exist; but even at the best, thousands of years must elapse before that Messianic age. Meanwhile nations live side by side in a state of relative peace, which is based chiefly on the fundamental equality between them. . . . But it is different with the people of Israel. This people is not counted among the nations, because since it was exiled from its land it has lacked the essential attributes of nationality, by which one nation is distinguished from another. . . . True, we have not ceased even in the lands of our exile to be spiritually a distinct nation; but this spiritual nationality, so far from giving us the status of a nation in the eyes of the other nations, is the very cause of their hatred for us as a people. Men are always terrified by a disembodied spirit, a soul wandering about with no physical covering; and terror breeds hatred. This is a form of psychic disease which we are powerless to cure. In all ages men have feared all kinds of ghosts which their imaginations have seen; and Israel appears to them as a ghost—but a ghost which they see with their very eyes, not merely in fancy. Thus the hatred of the nations for Jewish nationality is a psychic disease of the kind known as "demonopathy"; and having been transmitted from generation to generation for some two thousand years, it has by now become so deep-rooted that it can no longer be eradicated.

As one historian says of Pinsker's pamphlet, it is like "the prescription of the physician who has studied his own disease and is ready to plunge the scalpel into his own flesh."[9]

It was the suffering of his people that concerned Dr. Pinsker. Personally he was very successful. After receiving his M.D. from the University of Moscow, he returned to Odessa and practiced medicine. Shortly after the Crimean War came to an end, Odessa was full of soldiers suffering from typhoid fever. There was danger of an epidemic. He gave up his practice and devoted himself to the stricken soldiers. He was generously rewarded for this by Czar Alexander II. But the observation of his suffering brethren gave him no rest, and he searched for a cure for that.

Another physician who took a leading part in the Zionist movement from its inception, and a conspicuous figure at several Zionist Congresses, was Professor Max Mandelstamm (1838–1912). He was the leading ophthalmologist in Russia, a student of Graefe, Virchow, and Helmholtz, head of the eye clinic at the University of Kiev. Yet he continually kept his eye on all Jewish affairs and took a leading part in them.

When Herzl came on the scene of Jewish leadership, a world-famous Jewish psychologist was his guide and main supporter. Dr. Max Nordau (1849–1923) was one of the first to respond to Herzl's call, and he was practically second to Herzl in building up the organization. Here is what the great historian of Zionism, Sokolow, says of him:

Nordau placed his genius, his enthusiasm, and his powerful eloquence at the service of the Zionist idea and organization. His authority and influence in the propaganda of Zionism became the most powerful and influential force in the movement. Nothing could surpass the overwhelming logic and the admirable spirit of his speeches, pamphlets, essays, and articles. From the very beginning he played the part of a great leader with splendid confidence, inspiration, and dignity. No Zionist has exercised a stronger or a loftier influence by sheer strength of character and sound judgment. No orator or writer in modern times has so forcibly portrayed the great tragedy of his people as he has in his speeches at the Zionist Congresses, and none has voiced so eloquently the claims and hopes of his nation. He had always a message to deliver, and delivered it always effectively. He helped to make Zionism a world-wide movement, with an appeal not only to the Jewish people, but also to other nations. His forcible eloquence and untiring zeal in the service of Zionism are generally known. Nor does his public activity exhaust his services to the cause. He gave much useful advice to Herzl, who never undertook anything of importance in Zionist politics without consulting him. Nordau exercised enormous influence during the whole period of Herzl's and Wolffsohn's presidency, and is still doing so at the present moment. A man of great literary and journalistic achievement, with extensive associations and wide interests, a champion of all great causes of humanity and justice, zealously engaged in various domains of human thought, he has always placed

his time, his pen, and his matchless eloquence at the service of
Zionism.[10]

Herzl also found support in a number of other great physicians, among them, Waldemar Mordecai Haffkine, member of
the Pasteur Institute, who afterwards made a great name for
himself by his important work in India, and Alexander Marmorek, another worker in the Pasteur Institute, who was one of
the earliest of modern Zionists. Alexander and his two brothers
were the principal advocates of the national idea in academic
circles. For several years Alexander Marmorek served as president of the French Zionist Federation. He was one of the
founders of the *Echo Sioniste*. Marmorek was decorated with the
Cross of the Légion d'Honneur.

In the United States was Dr. Aaron Friedenwald (1836–1902),
professor of diseases of the eye in the College of Physicians and
Surgeons in Baltimore, president of the Medical and Chirurgical
Faculty of Maryland (1889–90), and a member of the medical
staff of a number of hospitals. At the same time he was one of the
most active members of all the local and national Jewish organizations. He was one of the founders and vice-president of the
Jewish Theological Seminary Association, the Jewish Publication
Society, and the Federation of American Zionists. But he did
more than that. In 1898 he visited the Holy Land to study the
conditions of the Jewish colony and to be an eyewitness to the
Jewish Renaissance.

It was during the same period that a Jewish physician,
single-handed, without any financial assistance, laid the foundation for the Jewish National Library in Jerusalem. I am referring
to Dr. Joseph Chasanowich of Bialystok. In 1928, when the
Zionist Organization took charge of the library, it consisted of
some 30,000 volumes, assembled chiefly through the zeal and
tireless effort of Dr. Chasanowich.*

It is in full keeping with the tradition of Jewish history that
when the work of restoring the Jewish homeland began in the
United States, Jewish physicians should take part and associate
themselves with the founding of a Hebrew University. A com-

---

*See below, p. 81, for a biographical study of Chasanowich.

mittee of prominent physicians is now engaged in raising funds to build the medical department of the Hebrew University.

The same tradition of Jewish physicans taking an important part in all Jewish movements holds in the rise of modern Hebrew literature. It was Judah Leib ben Joseph Kantor (1849–1915), who received his doctor's degree in Berlin, who started the first Hebrew daily newspaper, *Ha-Yom*, in St. Petersburg. In 1890 he was the associate editor of the *Ha-Meliz*. He also contributed to many other journals.

Another physician, Isaac ben Abraham Kaminer (1834–1901), who for fifteen years served as associate to Professor Mering at Kiev, was an able Hebrew writer and an especially talented satirist. His numerous contributions to periodicals, such as *Baraitot de-Rabbi Yizhak*, were very popular.

Another of the modern Hebrew satirists was Dr. Isaac Erter (1792–1851) of Brody, a graduate of the University of Budapest. He practiced in Galician towns. He was popular among the poor and needy, who found in him a kindly benefactor. Nearly a hundred years ago he urged the establishment of agricultural colonies for the employment and benefit of young Jews. But his fame rests chiefly on his satires, which according to the historian Graetz resemble in many ways those of Heinrich Heine. The following is a quotation from one of his most attractive and stinging satires, called *Gilgul Nefesh*.

It is the story of the many adventures of a soul during a long, earthly career; how it frequently passed from one body into another, how it had once left the body of an ass for that of a physician. The soul gives the author the following six rules, by observing which he will succeed in his profession—the Golden Aphorisms:

1. Powder your hair white, and keep on the table of your study a human skull and some animal skeletons. Those coming to you for medical advice will then think your hair has turned white through constant study and overwork in your profession.

2. Fill your library with large books, richly bound in red and gold. Though you never even open them, people will be impressed with your wisdom.

3. Sell or pawn everything, if that is necessary, to have a carriage of your own.

4. When called to a patient, pay less attention to him than to those about him. On leaving the sickroom, assume a grave face, and pronounce the case a most critical one. Should the patient die, you will be understood to have hinted at his death; if, on the other hand, he recovers, his relations and friends will naturally attribute his recovery to your skill.

5. Have as little as possible to do with the poor; as they will only send for you in hopeless and desperate cases, you will gain neither honor nor reward by attending them. Let them wait outside your house, that passers-by may be amazed at the crowd waiting patiently to obtain your services.

6. Consider every medical practitioner as your natural enemy, and speak of him always with the utmost disparagement. If he is a student of history dabbling in the annals of the past, say his work is alien to the practice of medicine. If he be young, you must say he has not had sufficient experience; if he be old, you must declare that his eyesight is bad, or that he is more or less crazy, and not to be trusted in important cases. When you take part in a consultation with other physicians, you would act wisely by protesting loudly against the previous treatment of the case by your colleagues. Whatever the issue may be, you will always be on the safe side.

Another Hebrew writer and contributor to Russian and Hebrew periodicals was the Russian physician Judah Leib ben Israel Katzenelson (1846–1917), who wrote under the pen name of Buki ben Yogli. He was graduated from the Imperial Medical Academy in St. Petersburg in 1877. He took part in the war against Turkey and was decorated twice by the Czar. He wrote a book on medicine in the Talmud entitled *Ha-Talmud ve-Ḥokmat ha-Refu'ah* and a novel, *Shirat ha-Zamir*.

Even in the new Palestine of today, the poet laureate is a physician.* From Judah Halevi to the present time, there has been a golden tradition of the Jewish physician playing on the Hebrew lyre.

Even a superficial study of Jewish history fills one with amazement and pride at the achievements of the Jewish physician. Not only did he distinguish himself in his art and science, but he continuously shouldered the task of furthering the progress of his people in its various ramifications. When the

*Dr. Savitz is referring to the Hebrew poet Saul Tchernichowsky (1875–1943) (ed.).

student of history confronts these intellectual giants, this feeling of pride gives way to one of humility and meekness.

NOTES

1. H. Graetz, *History of the Jews* (Philadelphia, 1894), vol. 3.

2. *Selected Poems of Jehudah Halevi,* trans. Nina Salaman (Philadelphia, 1924), p. 3.

3. There are Hebrew MSS of the *Canon* from the fifteenth century, as well as a complete Arabic MS of 1309, in the Hyams Collection.

4. Levi ben Gershom, *To'aliyyot* [Summaries of ethics] (Riva di Trento, 1570), in the author's collection.

5. Meyer Waxman, *A History of Jewish Literature* (New York, 1930).

6. Levi ben Gershom, Commentary on the Pentateuch (Mantua: Dr. Abraham Conat, 1476), in the Hyams Collection of the Boston Medical Library.

7. Cecil Roth, *A Life of Manasseh Ben Israel* (Philadelphia, 1934).

8. *Biblia Hebraica* (Amsterdam: Manasseh Ben Israel, 1635).

9. M. Raisin, *History of the Jews in Modern Times* (New York, 1919), p. 398.

10. Max Nordau, *History of Zionism* (London, 1919).

Jewish Medical Historians

The Jews are a historical people, not only in the sense that they have a continuous recorded history of nearly four thousand years, but also in that they possess a historical sense. This is perhaps a factor in their survival in spite of all the persecution and hardships to which they are subjected. They do not succumb to isolated phenomena. As a group they are neither dazzled nor blinded by sudden flashes of bright light nor crushed by total darkness. As an astronomer does, they sense that if an eclipse comes it will also pass. From their earliest recorded documents they reveal the tendency not to stop and look at one isolated still picture—they like to see the entire moving panorama in motion in time and space. "What comes before and what follows" is a common idiom in Hebrew—*Ma lefanim ma le'aher*.

Their very Book reveals that same trend. It commences with the words "In the beginning God created heaven and earth" and ends with a number of prophecies dealing with the distant future, "and it shall come to pass in the end of days."

The Hebrew language, from one point of view, has no present tense. It has a declension for the past tense and a declension for the future tense and uses merely a participle for the present tense. For what we call the present tense does not, in reality, exist. It is so momentary that it is either already in the past or it is yet to come. So too the people—like their language—live in the

First published in *Victor Robinson Memorial Volume: Essays on Historical Medicine.*

past with their eyes focused on the future. The Hebrew language reveals another characteristic. The use of one letter, *vav*, meaning "and," before a verb, changes its tense from the future to the past. This is known as the "*vav* conversive." In a sense it is very significant and symbolic. A people delves into its past, then the future or what is destined to come—becomes clear and they can read it like episodes of the past. In other words, a knowledge of history is a prophylactic against suffering repetition. As the last decade has shown, in spite of all the gruesomeness and barbarism of the age, the Jews survived, for they thrived on the glory of their past and their high hopes for a future that will be brighter. The Jews know that tyrants come and go. Tyrants have succeeded in liquidating a large number of their people, but never in crushing their hopes and instilling in them a spirit of defeatism.

The purpose of this paper is to show how this historical sense is revealed among a number of Jewish physicians and lay scholars who devoted their energies to medical history. Here is a branch of the art and science of medicine to which one is drawn by no thought of compensation but merely an inner urge—for the mere love of it. We shall also show how in some countries such men were the first to lay a foundation for the study of medical history.

The study of medical history has been for years mainly in the hands of German and French writers. So we shall start with those countries. The study of medical history was introduced in Vienna by an Austrian-Jewish physician who was also a Persian scholar, Franz Romeo Seligmann (1808–92). He received his M.D. degree from the University of Vienna in 1830. In 1869 he was appointed professor of medical history at his alma mater. In 1832 he published, in Vienna, *De Re Medica Persarum*, a translation and interpretation of the oldest Neo-Persian manuscripts on medicine.

In Berlin the study of medical history was introduced by Julius Leopold Pagel (1851–1912). After getting his M.D. degree at the University of Berlin in 1875, he established himself as a busy practitioner and medical writer in the capital city. In 1898 he received the title of professor of medical history at the University of Berlin. He was a prolific writer and editor. After 1885 he was assistant editor of Hirsch's *Biographisches Lexikon*. He was editor of *Deutsche Aerzte Zeitung* and *Biographisches Lexikon hervorragender Aerzte des Neunzten Jahrhunderts* (Berlin and Vienna, 1901), an encyclopedic history of medicine and a monumental piece of work. With Dr. Neuburger he published *Handuch der Geschichte der Medizin* (1902–5).

Professor Max Neuburger (1868–1955) was a Viennese specialist in nervous diseases. He was professor of the history of medicine at the University of Vienna (1904–38). In addition to his scientific work in his specialty, Neuburger published a number of historical monographs. He started as a collaborator of Dr. Pagel. He also published a history of medicine which was translated into English by Ernst Playfair under the direction of Sir William Osler. Professor Neuburger gained for himself a reputation for accuracy and scholarship. Dr. Garrison called him the "veteran" in medical history and outstanding in eminence among the active modern authors of works in this field. In 1939, as a refugee from his native land, he settled in London, where he continued his research until his retirement in 1948.

August Hirsch (1817–94) was professor of medicine at the University of Berlin. He was the author of the monumental *Handbook of Historic-Geographic Pathology* (1860–64). This work on the geographical distribution of disease has been translated into English and has become the standard textbook for physicians, particularly for those practicing in the tropics. One critic said: "For sheer painstaking labor Hirsch's book has never been equalled!" Dr. Hirsch sat on several commissions which investigated cholera and other epidemics.

August W. Henschel (1790–1886) was the son of the famous Breslau obstetrician Elias Henschel (1755–1839). He was a distinguished physician and botanist. His *Sexualität der Pflanzen* attracted considerable attention in the world of science, but he is best known for his research in the history of medicine. He edited *Janus* (Breslau, 1846–48) a journal dedicated to the history and literature of medicine.

Dr. Wilhelm Ebstein (1836–1912), professor of medicine at the University of Goettingen, an authority on malnutrition, wrote on medicine in the Bible and the Talmud. But the most exhaustive and monumental work in that field was written by a physician and medical writer in Berlin, Dr. Julius Preuss. His *Biblish-talmudische Medizin* (1911) will remain a monument to his name. It is still the outstanding work in the field.

Another important work on medicine in the Talmud was written in Hebrew by the Russian-Jewish physician Judah Leib Katzenelson (1846–1917). This prominent physician and author wrote under the pen-name Buki ben Yogli. He wrote poems and novels, both in Russian and Hebrew. His works are distinguished for their biblical style and their power of description. Being well versed in medicine and the Talmud, he was able to enrich considerably the medical terminology of the Hebrew language. But his principal works on talmudical medicine, are *Remaḥ Evarim* and *Ha-Talmud ve-Ḥokhmat ha-Refu'ah*.

Research on medicine in the Talmud was also done in the French language. Mr. Israel M. Rabbinowicz (1818–93) was born in Russia but settled in Paris in 1854. He was a great talmudical scholar and translator. He wrote Hebrew, Polish, French, and Latin grammars. He translated much of the Talmud into French. Among his other Talmud works he wrote *La Médecine du Talmud*. He also wrote another medical work, *Traité des poisons de Maimonide*.

Another French scholar who contributed to the history of the Jews in medicine was Eliakim Carmoly (1802–75). His real name was Goschel David Behr. The name Carmoly had been borne by his family since the fourteenth century. He was versed in French, German, and Hebrew and was employed at the Paris National Library. Afterwards he became rabbi in Brussels, whence he returned to Frankfort to devote himself to Jewish science. He wrote biographies of many scholars and a history of Jewish physicians (Brussels, 1849), which was translated into English. He edited the itineraries of early Jewish travelers. However, as he was not a trained physician, his statements are not always accurate.

But the most outstanding, and scholarly work in the field of the history of medicine, and of Jewish contributions in particular, was done by one of the greatest medical archivists, bibliographers, and orientalists, Moritz Steinschneider (1816–1907). He was born in Prosnitz, Austria, but later, being involved in the Kossuth rebellion, he had to leave his country. In 1848 he became a Prussian citizen and settled in Berlin. He was invited to Oxford, where he compiled, in Latin, his masterly catalogue of the Hebrew books and manuscripts at the Bodleian (1852–60). One could gain fame and immortality from this tremendous work alone. On his return to Berlin he became a lecturer in a Jewish school. From 1869 he was assistant librarian of the Berlin Royal Library. But his literary activities occupied every moment of his time, and one wonders how one man could accomplish so much in one life. His articles in Hebrew, Italian, Dutch, French, English, and Latin appeared in almost all the learned reviews of his day on such varying subjects as mathematics, Arabic translations, women in literature, and Christian Hebraists. He wrote authoritative studies on pseudo-epigraphic literature (1862), *Donnolo* (1868), etc. He published catalogues of the Hebrew manuscripts in Berlin, Munich, Hamburg, Leiden, etc. A list of his writings up to 1896, contributed by George Kohut to the Festschrift published in honor of his eightieth birthday, occupies thirty-nine large pages of small print. It comprises seventeen catalogues, forty independent works, sixteen contributions to the works of others, sixty-one sets of articles to encyclopedias and magazines, and twelve sets of articles in Hebrew journals. He crowned his labors with his great work, *Hebrew Translations During the Middle Ages* (1893).

Here was a man who devoted much of his life to the study of Jewish contributions to medieval science. He built monuments for himself and his people. No less than 2,168 Jewish physicians, who flourished between the period of the Dark Ages and the eighteenth century were of sufficient eminence to be recorded by him. His works are the tools of scholars who work at further research in various fields of learning.

In Holland we find the Dutch medical historian Abraham Hartog Israëls (1822–83). He received his M.D. degree in 1845 and started to practice in Amsterdam. In 1867 he became lecturer in the history of medicine and hygiene at the Athenaeum. In 1877 he was appointed assistant professor at the University of Amsterdam. He published numerous works on medical history and one on *Talmudic Gynecology* (1845).

In Italy we find Arturo Castiglioni (1874–1953), a descendant of a learned Italian-Jewish family and a graduate of the University of Vienna (1896). He was professor of medical history at Padua and later professor of the history of science at Perugia. Invited to Yale, he became professor of the history of medicine at Yale University School of Medicine, and retained this position until he returned to Italy in 1947. He is well-known for his *Storia della Medicina,* translated from the Italian by Dr. E. B. Krumbhaar, under the title *A History of Medicine.*

Iwan Bloch of Berlin (1872–1922) was one of the greatest authorities on sex problems, and was also known as a medical historian. His massive volume, *The Sexual Life of Our Time,* has long been a classic on the subject.

The same is true of Dr. Isidore Fischer of Vienna (1868–1943). Famous as a gynecologist, he was chief in that field at the Charitable Institute for Women in Vienna (1896–1921). He was at the same time privatdocent in medical history at the University of Vienna. He, too, made contributions to the history of medicine.

To the field of research in medical history in the English language, Dr. Charles Singer (1876–1960) of London devoted his energies. From 1920 he was professor of history of medicine at the University of London, and previously he was professor of the history of science at the University of California. He was chairman of a number of international scientific congresses and wrote on Greek biology, Greek medicine, the circulation of the blood, and a short history of medicine. Fielding H. Garrison once said of his work, "Charles Singer's studies on the history of contagion, microscopy and tropical medicine, and the illuminating essays of Sir William Osler are among the best that have been done in England."

Dr. Benjamin Spector (b. 1893), a native of New York and a graduate of New York University Medical School (1922), is not only professor and head of the department of anatomy but is also professor of the history of medicine at Tufts Medical School, Boston. He is a successful teacher in both. In addition to his academic activities and scientific research, he searched out and compiled all the facts and published the first history of Tufts College Medical School (1943).

We have in this country a group of eminent Jewish physicians and scholars who devote some of their time to medical history.

To them medicine is not only an art and a science but also a culture which has a long tradition. Eminent among this group was Dr. Harry Friedenwald (1864–1950) of Baltimore, professor of ophthalmology at the University of Maryland and generally active in Jewish higher education. He was a lover and collector of books, and published a number of articles in medical history. His papers were published in two volumes, *The Jews and Medicine* (1944).

There is also Dr. Herman Pomeranz of New York, whose writings cover a wide variety of subjects, including "Medicine in the Shakespearean Plays and Era," and "Dickens' Doctors."

Boston is proud of its cultured and genial physician, Dr. Hyman Morrison (1881—1962), a graduate of Harvard College and Harvard Medical School (1908) and clinical professor at Tufts College Medical School. He, too, was community-minded, and made notable contributions to the history of medicine. In 1927 he published a monograph on Carl Weigert, in which he gave a fine portrait of a great Jewish pathfinder in medicine. In 1928 he published an article containing many interesting facts on "The Early Jewish Physicians in America." In another paper he portrayed a pioneer of the medieval days, Isaac Judaeus. His style of writing is charming, simple, and scholarly.

Dr. Solomon R. Kagan (1889–1955) wrote numerous articles on medical, historical, bibliographical, and literary subjects published in Russian, German, Hebrew, and English. He was the author of a number of books, including *Jewish Contributions to Medicine in America* (1934), a most valuable source book of references.

Dr. Charles David Spivak (1861–1927) was professor of anatomy (1897–98) and professor of clinical medicine at the Denver School of Medicine (1900–1907). He contributed articles on medicine in the Bible and the Talmud.

Dr. Simon Flexner (1863–1946) was a research scientist and teacher and one of the leading bacteriologists of his time. He was director of the Rockefeller Institute for Medical Research from 1903 to 1935. His name is indelibly associated with the Flexner's dysentery bacillus and Flexner's antimeningococcus serum. He not only made a name for himself in the medical history of

America, but he also made a definite contribution to the history of medicine in America.

He was born in Louisville, Kentucky, on March 25, 1863, and received his M.D. degree from the University of Louisville in 1889. He pursued postgraduate studies at Johns Hopkins University. He then attended clinics in Europe at Strasbourg, Prague, Berlin, and later at the Pasteur Institute. He was professor of pathological anatomy at Johns Hopkins University from 1899 to 1903, and of pathology at the University of Pennsylvania. In 1903 he became director of the then newly established Rockefeller Institute. Many of his researches were carried out there. Recognition of his work came from almost every civilized country. He received honorary doctorates from many universities in America and Europe and distinctions from other learned bodies. Besides his many important contributions in pathological and bacteriological subjects, he also contributed to medical history. In 1941 he wrote, with his son James Thomas Flexner (b. 1908), a book entitled *William Henry Welch and the Heroic Age of American Medicine*. While written as a biography of the career of Dr. Welch, the beloved dean of American medicine in medicine's greatest age, this book is at the same time a carefully documented work of scholarship and an important contribution to the history of medicine.

His son James Thomas Flexner is well known for his widely read and much admired history of early American medicine, *Doctors on Horseback* (1937).

Dr. Simon's brother, Dr. Abraham Flexner (1866–1959), the educator, is well known for his reports and books on medical education in the United States, Canada, and Europe.

Another distinguished physician and scholar who contributed much to the history of medicine was Dr. Max Myerhof (1874–1945). He was born on March 21, 1874 of an old German-Jewish family in Hildesheim whose residence dated back to 1720. Scientists, physicians, and historians adorned both branches of his family. In 1903 he settled in Egypt as an ophthalmologist. He distinguished himself by his research and treatment in that field, particularly in the ocular diseases common in the Near East. His name became synonymous in Egypt with the restoration of sight to the blind. He also shed a great deal of light on the history of Arabic medicine. He soon mastered Arabic as well as other Semitic languages and began his researches in the original manuscripts. He brought to light a number of unknown documents, particularly the works of Maimonides, who practiced in Cairo nine hundred years previously.

In 1944, on Myerhof's seventieth birthday, the Hebrew University published a bibliography of his collected works comprising over three hundred publications. He was honored everywhere. In 1928 he received the honorary degree of Ph.D. at Bonn University. In 1930 he was offered the professorship of medical history at Leipzig University. But, a man of vision, he foresaw the dark clouds over Germany and the stifled atmosphere for free research, and he refused. As an ophthalmologist he brought light to the blind; as a medical historian he illuminated the history of science in the so-called dark Middle Ages.

In Philadelphia, born most appropriately, in the City of Brotherly Love, in the year 1892, we have Dr. Reuben Friedman, who received his M.D. degree from Temple University School of Medicine in 1916, and was associate professor of dermatology and syphilology at his alma mater. He was the foremost student in the country on the subject of scabies; his researches uncovered considerable new ground and his literary style was one of singular clarity and vigor. He was deeply interested in the building up of a medical library at the Hebrew University Medical School, and devoted much of his time and energy to the creation of a chair in the history of medicine at that institution.

Finally there is Dr. Victor Robinson (1886–1947) in whose honor this essay was written. He belongs to this noble group who have already developed a golden tradition. He was born in Russia and was educated in the United States. In 1917 he graduated from the Chicago College of Medicine and Surgery. In 1929 he became professor of the history of medicine at Temple University. He was an author and editor of high standing, a deep student of all things medical, all written in his inimitable style. He founded *Medical Life,* the first and only monthly journal of medical history in the English language. During the nearly two decades of his editorship, it served "as a cultural bridge between Europe and America." He was editor for twelve years of the *Medical Review of Reviews,* published by his brother Frederic. He authored many hundreds of articles and wrote more than a dozen books, including his famous trio of "stories"—of medicine, of anesthesia, and of nursing. He also founded the American Society for Medical History (1924) and the New York Society for Medical History (1939).

This list is by no means complete, yet it is sufficient to show how Jewish medical men and scholars have both laid the foundations and also continued to build that noble structure of medical history. We can see clearly that the achievement is international in character. Neither boundaries nor oceans can separate them: they all belong to one family, all engaged in a great, noble, and inspiring undertaking.

The To'elet Society of Amsterdam, 1815

When the Jew was forced to leave his country and take the wandering cane, in one hand, on his long journey through the Diaspora, he took a book with him in the other. As a result, Jews have had literary study groups, during their entire history— groups that studied the Torah, the Talmud, and the Midrash.

In Amsterdam, at the beginning of the nineteenth century, there was a group organized for the purpose of studying and spreading Hebrew culture among the local Jewish population, which in 1795 numbered about 20,052. Members of this club met: one of them would read an original paper, either in prose or poetry, essay or fiction. Several volumes of these papers were later published, and each book consisted of a collection of poems, essays, dramas, letters, etc. This society was similar to the Me'assefim of Germany, where several persons associated for the study and spread of Jewish literature. In Amsterdam they organized themselves under the name of "To'elet" (in Dutch, Tongeleth).

This society started in 1815 from an idea of one man, who called in some of his friends to organize the group. In 1820 it had forty-seven members, as well as twenty-two trainees who were preparing to become members. Future members were selected by invitation to read an original paper before the society in Hebrew. From the introductions to these papers, one can get the feeling and emotion as well as the honor involved in an invitation to join the group.

Presented before the "Amalgamated," Hanukkah, 1950. First published in *Jewish Forum*, August 1951.

In 1820 they published their first book, called *Bikkurei To'elet* (The First Ripe Fruit of To'elet). Within five years the first edition was completely sold out. In 1825 they published a second book, *Peri To'elet* (The Fruit of To'elet). Each book has the original autograph of the secretary. The second volume is signed Isaac Levi Milver. The first volume is found in the Hebrew collection of the Widener Library at Harvard University. The second volume was rescued from the Nazi loot and is in the library of the Hebrew Teachers College in Boston.

The purpose of this paper is to describe the society and review the papers that were published.

One of the founders and the main pillar of To'elet, as well as its poet laureate, was Samuel Mulder (1792–1862). His friends were Lehmans, Summerhaus, and Ullmann, who were also members of To'elet. They applied themselves to the study of the Hebrew language. In 1843 the University of Giessen conferred on Mulder the degree of Ph.D. In 1860 he was decorated with the Order of the Netherlands Lion. He was the first person to translate portions of the Bible into the Dutch language.

In 1820, on the fifth anniversary of To'elet, Mr. Samuel Mulder gave a lengthy report as chairman and organizer of the society. It is a philosophical report as well as a historical document (vol. 1). It not only gives the origin of the society but also throws light on the condition of the Jews in Amsterdam at that time.

Mulder begins his paper with the usual apologetics and expressions of awe. "Like metal in a smelting furnace," he says, "so is my heart melting within me as I think of my duties as chairman; namely, to report on the activities of the society." He then states that the main duty of man is to develop his mind, and in so doing he will develop himself in science and religion. Otherwise life is futile. Wealth and pleasures vanish, while the development of character is permanent. Religious knowledge, if it is to be developed at all, must be started in one's youth, else one would never attain it.

Mulder complains about a number of people who ask, Why teach children religion and implant faith within their heart in their youth; let them grow up and study the general sciences, and when they have reached maturity, then they will choose their own religion. But Mulder feels that, in spite of the fact that children are cultured in and taught French, German, the language of the Netherlands, art, music, and dancing, upon reaching maturity they will never come back to their religion. "When the fathers have eaten unripe fruit, the teeth of the children are put on edge."

Such were the thoughts that ran through Mulder's mind. He saw that our holy tongue was forgotten and realized that if one, perchance, could speak Hebrew, he was looked upon as a wild elephant brought from India, facts which made him very unhappy. His heart was heavy and his eyes were filled with tears at this realization, until he found two young men, Elhanan and David Benjamins, his dearest friends, who were interested in his idea, and together they planned a literary Hebrew society. Unfortunately, both of them died in 1815.

Later, Mulder found another friend, Moses, and they both sat down and worked out a plan for To'elet. After that time, many more members were added, so that in 1820 there were forty-seven members and twenty-two trainees (a branch of the club in which they prepared young men as future members). He concludes his speech by saying that he is very happy to transfer the leadership of this society to a great man, Zalman Hartenow. He ends his report by giving thanks to Jonah Benjamins, assistant secretary; Mair Lowenstein, Mulder's assistant; Saul Kaster; Alex Tal, first secretary; and Naftali Levi Kontiman, treasurer.

There is another paper, in volume 1, by Zalman Hartenow on "The Three Pillars of the World: Justice, Truth, and Peace," a saying based on *Pirkei Avot* 1:18, attributed to Simeon ben Gamaliel. This essay is philosophical in content. In it Hartenow tries to prove that there is a common denominator between these three abstract qualities. He starts with the usual lengthy introduction in flowery language for the honor paid him of asking him to write a paper. Although the paper was written over 130 years ago, to me it seems to be very appropriate at the present time. Hartenow says that, in justice, the judge must seek out the evidence like a general of the army, who before he besieges a city, sends out his intelligence and reconnaissance troops to gather all the possible information and weigh both sides. There must be neither prejudice nor favoritism. Justice is the great gift of God to man; without it man could not live in peace. That is why the Torah keeps on emphasizing the value of justice—neither to pity the poor nor to respect the great man; all must be equal before the bench of justice.

Truth is the second pillar which Hartenow explains. He states that there is no absolute truth; and here he uses a quotation from Maimonides, "that good and righteousness is the golden mean between two extremes"; so final truth is one extreme and absolute falsehood the other, and one must choose the mean of the two. Hartenow illustrates this idea by saying that if people were to say that his speech was the best in the world and that his words were pearls, he would know that it was just flattery. On the other hand, if they were to say that there was nothing in his speech, that it was full of nonsense, that would not be quite true either. The "mean" between these two statements would be that his speech was that of one who is still young, one who has had very little experience, but that there was something worthwhile in his speech. Then, Hartenow concludes, he would say that they were telling the truth.

This is equally true with peace. Life is a constant struggle; there can be no absolute peace, nor is it desirable to have a complete state of war. Therefore, peace is a state which is attained as a sort of compromise between these two forces. It seems that the period in which we are living at present is a tragic example of the truths Hartenow expounded—we neither have war nor do we have the equanimity of peace.

Most of the papers written by this group of Maskilim were in Hebrew, in the style of the Haskalah movement, or Hebrew Renaissance period. The style is full of *melizah,* "flowery language." Topics also were of diverse subjects: there is an essay by the secretary, Saul Kaster, on the "Virtue of Diligence and the Shame of Laziness."

Another paper is of interest to us. It is an etymological paper by Jacob, the son of Joshua Moses Polknov, delivered in 1822. It starts:

To my colleagues, members of To'elet, may they live forever! Not long ago, I was honored to join your society—men of truth, searching for the good and the wise. Today I was really honored by the heads of the society, the chairman, Samuel Mulder and Saul Kaster, secretary, who asked me to read before you a composition based on some research that I have done.

And modestly, he continues,

Since I am ignorant and not well versed, I shall trust to your kindness, so that if I have erred, you will correct me and bear no grudge against me. It is based on the Hebrew root *yorah*, from which is derived the Hebrew word Torah. It has four connotations: (1) throwing, (2) rain, (3) pointing with one's finger at something, and (4) teaching.

He concludes his paper with the thought that these four are derived from a common denominator which *yorah* connotates by "the bringing of something in the quickest and shortest way to its ultimate goal." And that is how we get the word "throwing," and the word "rain" (which comes straight down to the earth), and "pointing with one's finger toward something," and finally "to teach," which is to lead someone to certain truths. The word Torah also gets its meaning from the same source, for its purpose is to lead us to the right path and to the right goal in life.

Of the whole group of litterateurs there is one man who stands out; namely, the poet and scholar Samuel Mulder. He was not only the organizer of the group and editor of these volumes of essays but also a distinguished poet, and his poems were admired by his contemporaries. Most of his poems are found in the first volume. In the second volume there is an excellent poem entitled "Beruryah," about the revered daughter of Hananinah ben Teradyon and celebrated wife of Rabbi Meir. The episode in the poem is based on a comment on Talmud tractate *Avodah Zarah* by Rashi (fol. 18a), in which Rashi says: "Beruryah once jested sarcastically about the wise men who said that woman was fickle [Kiddushin 87]. Upon which Rabbi Meir replied, 'I swear that you will have to admit to the truth of their statements.' He then persuaded one of his disciples to seduce her, and after long persuasion she succumbed."

The poem starts with a discussion between Rabbi Meir (one of the most famous tannaim of the second century) and his famous wife. Daily he praised her beauty, but at the same time he would never fail to mention that, being a woman, she was fickle. She was a beautiful rose that had the usual thorn. Beruryah resented this and protested, enumerating the great women of the Bible. In order to settle the argument, Rabbi Meir persuaded one of his famous students, Ruiah, to see if he could steal her love away from her husband by flattery. Beruryah, the daughter of Hananinah, and a scholar in her own right, who could expound three hundred laws in one day and who had the courage to face the sudden death of her two sons and even comfort her husband in his distress, fell into the trap of flattery. Realizing what had happened, this great woman could not face life. Having been dishonored, she committed suicide.

This is a very dramatic and well-written poem. In the same footnote which gives its source, Mulder adds: "My intention and purpose in writing this poem was not for personal glorification but to uphold the gloriousness of our pure Hebrew language. I hope that all my efforts are not in vain, and that will be my reward."

His efforts were certainly not in vain, for not only did he contribute to the great Hebrew Renaissance, but he himself also occupies a place in Hebrew literature, and today, 130 years later, we recall his words. The members of this society were the Maskilim who started the Hebrew Renaissance in Holland. We have their names and brief sketches of their positions in Amsterdam.

Besides Samuel Mulder, the poet, there was Gabriel Polack (1803–69), the principal of a school. He was a talmudist and biographer and the author of several books. Moses Lehmans (1785–1832) was a Dutch educationist, a teacher of religion, who in 1828 was appointed teacher of mathematics in a school in Amsterdam. He was also the author of a biography of Maimonides.

I wish to conclude in the Ḥanukkah spirit, for no matter where Jews went or under what flag they lived, they always carried the Menorah with them, the symbol of Jewish culture. In some places they lit up a little candle, the rays of which were cast afar, and in some places this candle kindled a center of culture, whether in Holland with the To'elet society or in Germany with the Me'assefim.

In spite of all the persecutions and brutalities inflicted on

them, Jews have been able to survive, and it was as a result of
these little candles lit everywhere that we have reached the Third
Commonwealth, whose symbol is the Menorah.

Samuel Nehardea

One of the most celebrated physicians in the Talmud was Mar Samuel. He was a prolific author of medical dicta and a scholar who possessed and applied his vast medical knowledge. But this highly talented physician also was well known as a lawgiver, a judge, and an astronomer.

He was born about 180 in Nehardea, Babylon, and died there in 257. His father, a silk merchant, was himself a prominent scholar. As a boy Samuel displayed rare ability, and the father soon realized that he was unequal to the task of teaching his son. Samuel was sent to Nisibis, where Judah ben Bathyra had a famous college. In addition to Bible and the traditional law, Samuel studied the sciences, including medicine.

On his return to Nehardea he studied under Levi ben Sisi (a disciple of Judah ha-Nasi), who exerted a great influence on Samuel's development. His progress was so rapid that he was soon considered equal to his teacher. When Sisi left, Samuel accompanied his father to Palestine to study under Judah ha-Nasi (135–220), the editor of the Mishnah, who is referred to simply as Rabbi—master *par excellence*. It is recorded in tractate *Bava Mezia* (85b) that Samuel cured Rabbi of an eye infection.

Samuel Yarhina'ah was Rabbi's physician. Now, Rabbi having contracted an eye disease, Samuel offered to bathe it with a lotion, but he said, "I cannot bear it." "Then I will apply an ointment to it"; he said, "This, too, I cannot bear"; so he placed a phial of chemicals under his pillow and he was healed.

First published in *Tradition*, Fall 1973.

Rabbi was most anxious to ordain Samuel, but never did. Perhaps Rabbi could not assemble the ordination board, or possibly some members objected that Samuel devoted too much time to secular studies. So Samuel said, ironically,

Let it not grieve thee. I have seen in the Book of Adam [according to a legend, a book which God had shown to Adam containing the genealogy of the whole human race] in which it is written, "Samuel Yarḥina'ah will be called sage but not rabbi, and Rabbi's healing shall come through him."

That is why he is called Mar Samuel and not Rabbi.

On another occasion he healed Rabbi, but instead of praising Samuel, Rabbi scolded him. It is recorded in the Talmud that Samuel and Karna (both judges) were sitting by the bank of the Nehar Malka—the Royal Canal connecting the Euphrates and the Tigris rivers at Nehardea and Noh-oza respectively. Said Samuel to Karna, "A great man is coming from the west who suffers from stomach trouble, and the water is rising to give him a welcome. Go and smell his bottle [examine his knowledge—a humorous allusion to Karna's ability to judge wine]." So Karna met Rabbi and asked him several legal questions.

"What is your name?" asked Rabbi. "Karna." "May it be His will that a horn [*keren* is Hebrew for "horn"] shall sprout from between his eyes," retorted Rabbi. Subsequently Samuel took him into his house and gave him barley bread and a fish pie to eat and strong liquor to drink. (All this acted as a laxative, but he did not show him the privy that he might be eased. This was all part of the treatment.) "Rabbi cursed, saying, 'He who causes me pain may no sons arise from him,' and thus it was, for Samuel had two daughters" (*Shabbat* 108a).

The above episode is clarified thus—it seems to indicate that Samuel was practicing homeopathy, a system of therapy using doses of medicine that produce the symptoms of the disease treated. Rabbi cursed because his condition was made worse before it got better. So in a sense Mar Samuel Nehardea was sixteen hundred years ahead of Samuel Hanneman, who was the father of homeopathy.

From several references in the Talmud, Samuel seems to have been especially skillful in the treatment of the eye. He once spent eighteen months with a shepherd to study the eye diseases of animals. He developed an eye salve which was known as *"killurin of Mar Samuel"* and was in great demand. But he said, "Bathing the eye with cold water in the morning, and bathing the hands and feet in hot water in evening is better than all the eye salves in the world" (*Shabbat* 145).

Samuel also preserved the health of Rav. The story is told that there came before the *resh galuta* (exilarch) a young deer whose hind legs were broken. Rav examined the deer in the region of the juncture of the tendons and declared it to be permitted. He was about to eat a portion of it grilled when Samuel said to him, "Master, have you no fear lest it has been bitten by a snake?" "Then what is the remedy?" asked Rav. "Let it be put into an oven and it will expose itself." It was immediately put into an oven and it fell to pieces. Samuel applied the verse. "There shall no mischief befall the righteous" (Proverbs 2:21) to Rav, and Rav applied the verse "No secret troubleth thee" (Daniel 4:6) to Samuel.

As a physician Samuel claimed that he knew the cure of most ills. He energetically opposed the view that was then current, even in intellectual circles, that most diseases were due to the evil eye, *ayin ha-ra,* declaring that the source of all diseases must be sought in the noxious influence of the air and the climate upon the human organism. Today, when we are all attuned to the fear of air pollution, we can appreciate his warning nearly two thousand years ago.

Many of his aphorisms are practical as well as logical and scientific. He said that one was not to visit a patient until the fever had left him. Venesection, which was a common therapeutic measure in those days, was recommended by Samuel once in thirty days during middle age. What is most interesting is the statement recorded in the Talmud, "For Samuel, when he was bled [when he performed venesection], a dish of pieces of spleen was prepared." Was this not a forerunner of the liver therapy discovered by the Nobel laureate, Dr. George Richards Minot? Following venesection Samuel advised the patient to have food and to keep warm. R. Ḥiyya bar Avin said in the name of Samuel, "If one lets blood and catches a chill, a fire is made for him on the Tammuz [summer] solstice." A teak chair was broken up for

Samuel (*Shabbat* 129). Avlet (a Persian sage and astrologer and friend of Samuel) found Samuel sleeping in the sun, and said he to him: "O Jewish sage, can that which is injurious be beneficial?" "It is a day of bleeding," he replied, "and I require heat, etc."

Samuel believed that many diseases were due to the lack of cleanliness (*Shabbat* 133). He was very particular about touching food without washing his hands. It is stated that Samuel once found Rabbi eating with a cloth and assuming that he had not washed his hands, said to him, "Is it right to do so?" Rabbi replied, "I am very sensitive." He washed his hands but would not touch his food with his fingers and always wrapped a cloth around them (*Hullin* 107b). Samuel was also very careful to abstain from drinking water that had been standing uncovered (*Avodah Zarah* 30). Rav did not drink water from an Aramean's house. Samuel, on the other hand, would not drink water in the house of a widow. In the absence of the fear of the husband, he said, she would not necessarily keep the water covered. However, he drank water in the house of an Aramean because even if they are not particular about uncovered liquids, they are particular about cleanliness (so they will keep it covered for the sake of cleanliness).

Samuel traced the course of other illnesses to a disturbance in the regular mode of living. As he expressed it briefly: "A change of diet is the beginning of bowel trouble" (*Ketubbot* 110b). According to Samuel, it was necessary to lead a life of regularity adjusted to the cycle to which one was accustomed. In our jet age we can appreciate this because the inherent ability of creatures to anticipate and adjust to conditions in their normal surroundings is a most important asset in survival. For example, most people are in harmony with a schedule in which there are certain hours for sleeping and certain hours to be awake. If one travels by jet to another country, and the rhythm of waking and sleeping is changed, one experiences fatigue and difficulty in normal activity. We now understand that life is expressed as a continuous cyclic motion synchronized with itself and with the world around us.

In order to preserve one's health, Samuel also recommended that "up to the age of forty food is more beneficial; thereafter drink is more beneficial" (*Shabbat* 152). Modern medicine agrees with this. Also, "He who washed his face and does not dry it well, scabs will break out on him; what is the remedy? Let him wash it well in beet juice (or water in which vegetables were thoroughly boiled)." Among other aphorisms of his we find: "Sleep at dawn is like a steel edge to iron" (*Berakhot* 62); "All reptiles have a poisonous venom; that of a serpent is fatal, while that of other reptiles has no fatal effect." Samuel seemed to understand the principle of immunity. He said to Ḥiyya bar Rav:

Son of a scholar, come and let me tell you a good thing which your father Rav used to say. Thus said your father, "The reason why those swollen Arameans who drink that which is kept uncovered suffer no fatal consequences is because through eating abominable and creeping things their bodies become immune from it." (*Avodah Zarah* 31b)

Not only did Mar Samuel study diseases of the eye in animals, but he made other investigations. Notable among them was the experiment with *beiẓah trumita,* namely an egg boiled down to the size of a pill which, on being swallowed by the patient, passes through the body unchanged, carrying with it matter which helps the physician in making a diagnosis (*Nedarim* 6). As stated in the Talmud,

What is *beiẓah trumita?* Samuel said: "The slave who can prepare one is worth a thousand *dinari,* for it must be placed a thousand times in hot water, and a thousand times in cold water, until small enough to be swallowed whole. If one is ulcerated, it attracts the matter to itself, and when it passes out the doctor knows what medicine is required and how to treat the patient.

Samuel used to examine himself with a *kulha*—the stalk of some plant (which acted like *beiẓah trumita*)—a process which so weakened him that his household tore their hair in desperation (*Nedarim* 50).

The following episode indicates that Samuel was also a good epidemiologist. Once Samuel was informed that pestilence was raging among the inhabitants of Be-Ḥozai (the modern city of Khurzistan) and he ordained a fast. The people said to him, "Surely Be-Ḥozai is a long distance away from here [Nehardea]." He replied, "Would, then, a crossing prevent it from spreading?" In other words, travelers would carry the disease, as we have now learned in an era of world-wide transportation (*Hullin* 101).

Samuel also showed some skill as an embryologist: "A certain sac [embryo] was submitted to the master Samuel; he said, 'This is forty-one days old.' A formal investigation of the case proved that he was correct" (*Niddah* 30). As a physician he was meticulous about the care of the patient. He advised people not to visit a patient with a fever. As a sign of his profession he sometimes drew the figure of a palm branch as his signature.

After he had studied the Mishnah and the civil laws, Samuel returned to his native city, Nehardea. His reputation as a teacher of the law had preceded him and many pupils gathered about him. Mar Ukba, a former pupil, appointed him judge in the court of Nehardea. Samuel and Karna were called the "Judges of the Diaspora." His integrity as a judge is revealed by the soundness of his moral principles. He interpreted the verse "Thou shall take no bribe" (Exodus 23:8) to mean that not only may a judge not accept a bribe of money; but even a bribe of words is also forbidden. Mar Samuel was passing over a bridge when a man gave him his hand to support him. Mar Samuel asked the man, "Why?" The man replied that he had a suit pending. "Then," said Samuel, "I am disqualified in acting for you in this suit" (*Ketubbot* 105b).

Samuel was also known for his epoch-making contributions to the doctrines of Judaism. He declared that the law of the land where Jews reside is as binding on the Jews as their own law and that it is forbidden to deceive anyone, Jew or pagan (*Hullin* 94). He applied this rule strictly in his own dealings. Samuel was once crossing on a ferryboat and said to his attendant, "Reward the ferryman." He rewarded him, but Samuel became angry. Why was he angry? Abbaye said: "Because the attendant had a *trefa* hen and gave it to the ferryman, representing it as one that was ritually slaughtered." Rav said, "Because Samuel told him to give him [the Gentile] *ampaka* to drink, and he gave him mixed wine to drink, and the Gentile thought it was unmixed" (*Hullin* 94).

Samuel also stated that anyone who was not well versed in the laws of marriage and divorce should not officiate at a marriage ceremony. He was concerned with the social and economic condition of his people and declared that one should assist one's fellow man at the first sign of approaching difficulty so as to prevent trouble. As a physician he applied the principle of prevention to poverty just as to disease.

Mar Samuel also gained a reputation as an astronomer. The low-lying plain between the Euphrates and the Tigris had been the cradle of astronomy, but soon degenerated into the pseudo-science of astrology. Because of his Jewish education, which forbade the practice of divination and soothsaying (Leviticus 19:30), he occupied himself with astronomy in spite of the fact that he studied with the Gentile scholar Avlet, who was an astrologer. Samuel used to boast that he was as well acquainted with the ways of the skies as he was with the streets of Nehardea. He turned his knowledge of astronomy to a practical account; he drew up a fixed calendar for the festivals so that the Jews in Babylon did not have to depend on Palestine for the determination of the new moon. He was therefore also called Samuel Yeharnea (Hebrew *yarea,* the moon expert).

Samuel's logical mind and analytical power are to be found in his lore as well as in his laws. He seemed to stress that Jewish history has a moral and prophetic aspect; it teaches the virtue of morality. He said, "On the day Solomon married Pharaoh's daughter, the archangel Michael descended from heaven and stuck a great pole in the sea, which gathered mud about it. So the place became like a thicket of reeds and formed the site of Rome." The most obvious interpretation seems to be that Solomon's kingdom, a most glorious period, seemed destined for punishment, even though centuries away, when moral values started to crumble. For Rome, in 70 c.e., conquered and destroyed the Jewish state. As Rabbi Herman said: "God is long-suffering but he collects his due."

Mar Samuel was of an even temperament, avoiding enthusiasms and demonstrativeness. While his contemporaries believed that in the Messianic period all sorts of miracles would occur, Samuel propounded the view that every day would still follow its natural course, but that the subjection of Israel to foreign rulers would come to an end.

Some of his remarks indicate that he loved life—had *joie de vivre.* He said to Judah: "Keen disciple, make haste. Eat and drink, since the world from which we must depart is like a wedding feast" (*Eruvin* 54a). He also declared, "He who indulges in fasting is a sinner." Every festive occasion, he believed, should be enjoyed fully. "A wedding may not be held in a festival week because we do not mix one joy with another; and no mourning rites on the Sabbath." To enjoy life, one must not hustle and hurry. "Who forces time is pushed back by time; who yields to time finds time on his side" (*Eruvin* 136).

Mar Samuel had many admirable characteristics and many noble qualities. He was distinguished for his modesty, gentleness, and unselfishness. He had the humility of a true scholar. He said, "God exalts the self-humbling and humbles the self-exalting" (*Eruvin* 13b). Furthermore, "Greatness flees from him who seeks it and follows him who flees from it." He was very sensitive about the dignity of man and careful not to insult others. "Who stigmatizes others does so with one's own blemishes" (*Kiddushin* 70). He was ever ready to subordinate his own interests to those of the community. He said, "A man may never exclude himself from the community, but must seek his welfare in that of society (*Berakhot* 49b).

Such was this man of immense knowledge; judicial mind, humble and kind, and of noble character. In Hebrew there is a word that describes a man in whom all is contained—universality of knowledge and nobility of character—*ish eshkolot*. It is a play on the words *ish shehakol bo*—he is like a cluster of golden grapes. Such a man was Mar Samuel.

Abraham Portaleone: Italian Physician, Erudite Scholar, and Author

For centuries the Jews maintained a continuous line of medical practitioners. Some families were famous for producing several generations of prominent physicians as well as Hebrew scholars. From such a family came the distinguished physician and erudite scholar of Mantua, Abraham Portaleone. He was a descendant of a prominent Jewish family of northern Italy, which probably derived its name from the quarter of Portaleone situated in the vicinity of the ghetto of Rome. His family had lived in Italy for more than two centuries. His great-grandfather was knighted by the king of Naples in 1438 for his medical services to the king.

The autobiographical sketch of this extraordinary personality reveals many unexpected facets of his life. The following are the words recorded at the end of his famous *Shiltei ha-Gibborim* (The Shields of the Brave), published in Mantua in the year 1612:

Remember noble reader that I was born at midnight, Saturday, in the month of Nisan in the year 1542 to my noble father, the crown of my

First published in *Panminerva Medica,* December 1966.

head, David Portaleone, famous among physicians until the day that he
was called to heaven. It is he who gave me my early Hebrew education.
It is he who taught me to read the Hebrew language and study its
grammar, and with whom I also studied the Pentateuch, the Prophets,
and the Sacred Writings. Then, when I left the city of Boliva, I studied
with Jacob Fano, of blessed memory, an Italian rabbi and poet. But God
punished us and there was a fire in the city, so I returned and studied
with Judah Provençal and with other great physicians and
philosophers. Then I matriculated in the University of Padua, where I
studied the works of great physicians and philosophers, the works of
Aristotle, Galen, as well as the works of other famous Arabic physicians.
I studied there until I was given the title Doctor of Philosophy in
Medicine. At the same time I never abandoned to study the law of God.
In the month of Nisan in the year 1563, I was accepted in the College of
Physicians and Philosophers. In 1563, on the nineteenth day of the
month Elul, my colleagues, the physicians of Mantua, accepted me as a
member and gave me license to practice like the rest of them in Mantua
and its vicinity. My noble father, the crown of my head of blessed
memory, became old and advanced in years. His health failed him, so
our God gave me the opportunity to fill his place. I was taught a great
deal about various diseases in medicine and surgery.

I was also taught to circumcise children and bring them into the
covenant of our father, Abraham. By the sixth day of the month
Marḥeshvan in the year 1566, I have already circumcised 360 children.
In a diary I recorded the name of the father and mother of the child,
the day of the circumcision according to our calendar, the portion of
the week, the names of the godfather and godmother, and if it
happened to be a firstborn son, I also recorded the topic of the sermon
delivered on that day and the weekly portion read in the synagogue.

After the death of my father, the crown of my head of blessed
memory, I was treating Jews and Gentiles, lords and nobles. But as a
result of that, I neglected the study of the Torah. I composed a book in
Latin for physicians consisting of various responses in Latin for
doctors. In one book I composed and collected all the remedies for
various ailments as well as those diseases that require surgery.

That book is in the hands of my son, the physician David, may God
preserve his health. By the request of our lord, his excellence, the Duke
of Mantua, I composed, by his command, a book in Latin in which I
discussed the use of gold, whether it is of therapeutic value as some of
the earlier physicians claimed. This was published in the year 1584. But
as a result of that I neglected the study of the Torah, for that the hand

of God was on me. In the month of Tammuz, in the year 1605, God punished me, and I became paralyzed. I could not move my legs or arms like the rest of the people. I became more like a dead person.

During the last part of the year 1606 during my sickness, I prayed to God and repented for my sins, and I decided to correct the sins I had committed. I composed for my children a compendium of the Bible, the Mishnah, and the Midrash with all its legends as well as the order of the services for the rest of the year. I have not done this for my personal glory, but to atone for my sin of neglecting the study of the law, and with my right hand I succeeded in completing the book *Shiltei ha-Gibborim*, ninety-two chapters.

This final testimony reveals a great many extraordinary facets of the period. Portaleone states that his body should be left for an interval of three days, exactly seventy-two hours, before burial. This is unlike the Jewish tradition.

We also learn that his son, David, obtained his degree of philosophy on March 19, 1596; at the same time he also obtained a license from Pope Clemens VIII. On December 15, 1599, he was accepted in the College of Physicians.

Abraham Portaleone left his entire library of books in Hebrew, Latin, and other languages to David. It is interesting that he lived seven years after this last testament.

In writing of this book, Abraham Portaleone enumerates ten foreign languages that he mastered; namely, Italian, Aramaic, German, Bohemian, Greek, Latin, Spanish, Arabic, Persian, and French. In his first chapter he speaks of his intense love and admiration of the Holy Land. He enumerates several reasons why that land is sacred. Then he describes in detail the structure of the Temple and the garments of the high priests; particularly of interest is the charge of the high priests to the soldiers before they go to war. He describes the breastplate and vestments of the high priests. On the breastplate were four rows of precious stones. In the first row were sardu, topaz, and emeralds. In the second row were carbuncles, sapphires, and diamonds. In the third row were opals, turquois, and amethysts. In the fourth row were chrysolite, onyx, and jasper. In each he gives the colors of the precious stones. He also gives the Greek and Latin equivalent for the name of each particular stone. He also gives the etymology of the Hebrew word for it. Here is a great deal of material for those interested in the study of precious stones.

Professor David Kaufman (1852–1899) was the possessor of a large library which contained many valuable manuscripts. Among them was a manuscript which contained the will of Dr. Portaleone. The following is a description of the will, together with a biographical sketch:

The circumstances that may have inclined Portaleone, Physician-in-Ordinary to Guglielmo and Vincenzo, Dukes of Mantua and Montferrat, to draw up this will, are not known. Jewish literature owes one of his most notable contributions the Archaelogical Work, *Schilte-Ha-Giborim*, during the epidemic which suddenly broke out in July, 1605. Paralyzed in his left side, probably the after effect of an apoplectic seizure, and deprived for nearly a year of the use of his limbs, Portaleone, who combined the intensest piety with the widest culture, examined himself while lying helpless on a sick bed, in order to discover the special sin which he was then expiating by his sufferings, and he found it, he thought, in his exclusive devotion to philosophy and medicine, and consequent neglect of Jewish studies. The monumental work to which he dedicated his energies on his recovery shows how nobly he fulfilled the vow he had taken in his illness. In a similar way, the will before us is a revelation of his innermost soul at a time when he believed his end was approaching. He has already escaped greater danger, and so he cherished now also the hope of complete recovery.

Once, on a Sabbath, the 25th of February, 1576, a desperado called Agostino, son of Raffaello, treacherously attacked him. He was struck on the head, but otherwise received no injury. Several lunges with a sword were made at him by his assailant but only his clothes were slit in sixteen places. He personally escaped unwounded, and did not even lose a single drop of blood. Enjoying the esteem of his co-religionists and honoured by his prince, who in a decree dated 15 May 1577, had conferred upon him the appointment of physician-in-ordinary, he had attained his sixty-third year, when a new danger reminded him of the frailty of human life, and decided him to draw up and publish his last will.

This will not only afford us an insight into its author's mental idiosyncrasies, but is also of extreme interest to the history of religion. When we take into account the struggles and controversies on the subject of hasty and premature burial, which continued to the close of the last century, when they finally prohibited them, it will be admitted that this will deserves to be emphatically quoted as an early and valuable protest against this outrageous practice. It was probably, first and foremost, Abraham's medical experience that induced him to so earnestly enjoin his children not to allow his remains to be committed to the dust till three days had elapsed after his decease. The nine points which form the body of the will are preceded by a confession, whose devotional spirit will be better appreciated when it is remembered that it was made by one of the most eminent physicians of his country, a descendant of physicians, whose great-grandfather had been knighted in 1438 for his medical services by Fernando, King of Naples. A legacy of five soldi to the Mantua Hospital is merely a formal precaution, the aim of which is to secure for his will the protection of the law.

His body is to be left unburied for an interval of three days, exactly seventy-two hours. Should this period be succeeded by Sabbath or Festival, when funerals are forbidden, the interment may take place earlier, but only after a rigorous post-mortem examination has proved beyond doubt that life was indeed extinct. If it will be found inconvenient to keep the corpse in the house during the three days, it should be conveyed to the cemetery mortuary, and there watched.

The grave is to be paved with stones, cemented with lime and gypsum, and enclosed by four walls, an ell high. At the corners, four marble pillars are to be erected to support a stone roof slanting in two directions, to allow the rain to run off. The coffin, with the lid not nailed down but simply covering it, is to be placed on the ground. Neither earth nor any other substance is to be strewn on it. The sepulcher shall be sufficiently wide to admit of a second coffin being placed next to his, should his surviving wife desire sepulture in the same vault. He impresses on his sons the duty of not giving way to overwhelming grief, and adjures them scrupulously to carry out his directions and to respect them as expressing his innermost convictions. Ten ducats are to be given after his death to the poor fund in fulfillment of an old vow, and alms are to be distributed, worthy of his and his children's station.

His widow is to remain mistress of the home. She is not to be restricted in any way, or bound to render an account of her doings to anyone. The sons, who are to provide her with maintenance, clothing and thirty scudi annually for her private use, are exhorted to treat her with the utmost respect. The father expresses the hope that they will be a comfort to her in her bereavement, and allow her to want for nothing to which she has been accustomed. If disharmony should unfortunately break out among them, she shall be allowed to choose her home with any of her children without prejudice to the obligations her sons owe toward her. She shall also have the right to claim her dowry and dispose of it at her pleasure. The testator expressly requests her not to remove her residence from Mantua.

To each of his granddaughters, Bella, Esther, Sara, and Diamond, issue of his daughter Rebecca and her husband, Elieser Montalboto, he bequeaths a dowry of 125 scudi. In case of death of any of these grandchildren, the surviving sisters become her heirs; should his daughter survive all her children, the whole amount is to be paid to her.

He recommends his sons to work in partnership, and at least not to divide the estate till their youngest brother shall have reached his twentieth year, i.e., attained his majority. When a dissolution becomes inevitable, the private property each brother brought in by marriage to the estate shall first be deducted, and it shall then be conscientiously divided. To his son David, who obtained his doctorate in philosophy and medicine at Padua, on the 19th of March, 1596, receiving his license to practice—which as a Jew, he had to seek specially from Pope Clemens VIII—on the 13th of November, 1598, and was accepted, on the 15th day of December, 1599 by the College of Physicians at Mantua, Abraham leaves his entire medical and philosophical library, both the Hebrew and Latin works in these departments, as well as books written in other languages. To this portion of the estate the other brothers shall have no claim. The remainder of the Hebrew library, however, is to be equally divided among the three brothers. Eleasar, named after his great-grandfather Lazzaro, is asked to continue his interest, even after the division of the estate, in the affairs of his youngest brother, Jehuda, who had taken to silk manufacture. Finally, he enjoins his children not to stop the allowance he used to make to his sister Rebecca, Isaac Putino's wife.

The witnesses who appended their signatures to this document were men of note; one, Jedidiah Salomon b. Abraham Norzi, eminent in Masoretic study and research, the famous author of *Minhat Shai*, was Abraham's friend. Portaleone gratefully mentions in his work (fol. 102a) that he is indebted to him for a list of the psalms recited on the various Sabbaths and festivals, which his grandfather, the Gaon Norzi, had compiled.

Elieser Provinciale [Provençal], the second witness, was the son of the distinguished talmudist, philosopher, and physician whom Portaleone, at the end of his book, names as his teacher. Both Norzi and Provinciale belonged to the Mantua Rabbinate on the 10th of July, 1605, the date when this will was drawn up.

Abraham Portaleone recovered from his illness, and lived seven years longer. One part of the will was rendered nugatory—that, namely, in which Portaleone's solicitude for his wife's welfare is so tenderly exhibited. He was engaged in counting, for the second time, the words of Scripture for his great archaeological work, when his life's companion, Sara, daughter of the distinguished Moses Cividale, was taken from him, in her 59th year, on Friday, the 5th day of Passover, 1611. That she, the younger, would survive him, had been assumed by him as a certainty, but it was otherwise fated. Abraham followed her on the 29th of July, 1612, in his 71st year. His sepulcher in the Jewish cemetery at Mantua, concerning which he left such minute directions, has disappeared. This circumstance confers upon his grandson an additional title to our gratitude for having preserved his ancestor's last will, thus affording another illustration of the truth expressed in Solomon's Song (8:6) that "Love is as strong as Death."

Dr. Abraham Portaleone was fortunate to live at the height of the Italian Renaissance. The immortal genius Michelangelo 1475–1564) lived twenty-two years after Portaleone's birth; Leonardo da Vinci died about twenty-three years before.

In medicine, too, it was a great golden period at that time in Italy. Andreas Vesalius (1514–1564) received his M.D. in 1543, and wrote one of the great books of the sixteenth century, *De humani corporis fabrica*. His contemporary at the university was Gabriello Fallopio (1523–1562), who discovered or described the chorda tympani, the sphenoid sinuses, various facial muscles and nerves, as well as the organs of the female pelvis. Another contemporary of Portaleone was the great Italian anatomist and embryologist, Fabrizio de Aquapendente (1537–1619).

The home of Dr. Portaleone was a meeting place for Jewish scholars. In the sixteenth century, Jewish students from Poland were not admitted to the Amsterdam University. So a number of Jewish students from Poland studied at the famous University of Pauda in Italy, among them Dr. Samuel de Lima, his family had been exiled from Spain, its native country, and moved to Amsterdam, where Samuel was born in the second half of the sixteenth century. Since Jewish students were not admitted to the Amsterdam University, Samuel studied at the University of Pauda, which was famous for its scholars, physicians, philosophers, and naturalists. While in Italy, Dr. Samuel de Lima maintained contact with the eminent Jewish physician, Abraham Portaleone. At the end of the sixteenth century, Dr.

Samuel de Lima went to Poland and settled in Posen. He died in 1626.

The Hebrew language, on the other hand, was a magic carpet to Dr. Portaleone on which he traveled many centuries back and was able to study the construction of the Temple and the paraphernalia of the high priests, as well as the Hebrew literature that extended over two thousand years.

Dr. Ephraim Luzzatto: Physician and Poet

Ephraim Luzzatto was born in 1729 in San Daniele in northern Italy. The son of a prominent Jewish Italian family, he was also known by his Italian name, Angelo. Jews have the fine art of adapting to the culture of the land in which they reside, and so Angelo, born and educated in Italy, where the air is filled with song, sang and composed songs. But the Jew, though toiling in other gardens, seldom forgets his own vineyard, and Ephraim the Jew studied the Bible and the Hebrew language, and acquired a rich and sensitive Hebrew vocabulary.

Medicine seems to have been the intellectual outlet of his family. His grandfather, Isaac Luzzatto, received his medical degree on February 20, 1687, and Isaac's son, Raphael, was graduated on May 4, 1717. Raphael had three sons—all were physicians and graduates of the University of Padua. Ephraim's brother Isaac, also a famous poet, received his degree on July 29, 1747. So it was natural that Ephraim, at the early age of thirteen, matriculated at the university in 1742. He received his M.D. degree in May 1751.

He practiced for some years in Padua, in Livorno, and in Trieste, as well as in other Italian cities. There were large Jewish communities in each of these cities, and he became their beloved physician. On various auspicious occasions he dedicated poems

First published in *Rhode Island Medical Journal,* August 1973.

53

in their honor, often written on prescription blanks. The chief characteristic of his poetry was its light and natural tone.

Luzzatto wrote poems commemorating events in the life of the community, sometimes even trivial events, such as the birth of a son in the family of a friend who had three daughters. In general, he viewed life in a playful mood. But as is characteristic of Hebrew writers and poets nurtured on the Bible, he developed a deep urge for perfection and aimed his sarcastic arrows at physicians who he felt had undignified bedside manners. The following is a free translation of a stanza of one of his poems:

> If the patient was a beautiful dame
> To sooth her pain hours took;
> But if she were old and lame
> Sufficient was one minute look.

He also produced a simple guide to good living:

> Enjoy wealth, its loss do not despair,
> Be ever wise, do not abuse the uncouth;
> To everyone be pleasant and fair,
> Adore the aged and love youth.

In a more serious mood, he composed a stormy poem, "Kez kol bosor," in which he bewailed the vanity and brevity of human life. He advised against pursuing worldly pleasure for tomorrow, for one does not know what the day will bring.

Like the physician, poet, and philosopher Judah Halevi (1085–1142), whose best known and most beloved poems were inspired by a yearning for Zion, Luzzatto wrote three poems in which he poured out his heart, bewailing the desolation of Zion and praying for its restoration. In a poem entitled "Lema'an Zion lo echshi" ("For the sake of Zion I shall not keep silent") he wrote:

> A jackal am I for wailing Zion's desolation;
> No rest for me until its restoration.

Dr. Luzzatto was a restless person in his youth; he married

young, and his wife died shortly thereafter. This was, perhaps, one of the reasons that he moved to London in 1763, where he was an attending physician at the hospital of the Portuguese Jewish community for thirty years. But even though he was fully occupied with his work, he managed to continue his writing of Hebrew poetry. He was married to medicine, but poetry was his mistress.

In 1768 Luzzatto published his collection of poems titled *Elleh Benei ha-Ne'urim* (These Are the Children of Youth). The title implies that the poems are the children of the poet. Only one hundred copies were printed, for distribution among his friends rather than to the reading public. He left many more poems in manuscript, a boxful it is claimed; but the person who came into their possession did not understand their value, and they were burned.

In 1792 Luzzatto decided to leave London and return to Italy, his native land. He was old and sick and probably felt that his days were numbered. Since he was a widower, he lived alone and longed to return to his home and die among his friends. He went home by way of Lausanne, Switzerland, so that he could consult with the world-famous practitioner André Tissot (1728–97). But his condition worsened, and death met him on the way. Luzzatto died in Lausanne in 1792 at the age of sixty-three. Luzzatto left a will, which according to the historian Cecil Roth he wrote just before he left London for his return to Italy. In it he disposed of his small property. He had a devoted housekeeper, who took care of him faithfully, and in his will he remembered her and others who had befriended him. The following passages from his will are of interest:

London 17th April 1792

I Angelo Luzzatto, upon the point of setting off for Italy seriously reflecting that Death bears universal sway and seizes the poor victims everywhere judged it expedient to dispose of what little property I leave behind as follows:

To my dearly beloved housekeeper, Miss Ann Davis £300, as an acknowledgement for her kind assiduities and constant attachment to my person.

To Kempe Brydgges, Esqr. formerly a laceman in Bedford Street and in case of his decease, to his son, Kempe Brydges, Junr. Esqr., £ 200, as a grateful sense of the unparallelled kindness and unbounded assistance I have received from the old gentleman in all the troubles and difficulties I met with during a long period of time after my arrival in England.

To my brother Dr. Isaac Luzzatto of St. Daniel in Trinlia (Friuli) £150, and to the heirs of my late brother Menosta [Manasseh?] Luzzatto, £100. After these legacies are paid, it is my wish that my friends, Mr. N. Modigliani and Mr. P[eter] Burcan will accept £25 each, and kindly undertake the trust of executing this my last will. To the present Recorder of London, to Capt. Churchill, to Mr. Prince, to John Bradburne Esqr., to Mr. Sciaccalaza, and to my servant, Elizabeth Brewer, £10 each.

To Mr. P. Molini, of Woodstock Street, and to Judith Sympson of No. 8 Hemmings Row, £5 each.

Mr. Hughes, Mr. Foy and Mr. Levy, my good Executors clerks, and to Mrs. Mansell and T. Hall £5 each.

I leave the necessary sum for the payment of my arrears to the Portuguese Synagogue, and what might be left of money together with my household furniture, apparel, plate, linen and every article in my possession I leave to my beloved friend Miss Ann Davis to whom, as indeed all mankind perfectly resigned to my fate, I wish peace and happiness.[4]

Luzzatto's entire contribution was that he left also a tiny volume of Hebrew verse to make its niche in the temple of modern Hebrew literature.

NOTES

1. Jacob Fichmann, ed., *Shirei Ephraim Luzzatto* (Tel Aviv, 1942).
2. Meyer Waxman, *A History of Jewish Literature* (New York: Bloch, 1934), vol. 3, p. 134.
3. Cecil Roth, introduction and profile of Ephraim Luzzatto, in *Sefer Hayyim Schirmann* (Jerusalem, 1970), p. 369.
4. In a codicil to the will Luzzatto also left "to Miss Marianne Perrouet du Chateaux d'Oix dwelling at Lausanne a la rue Pallud, five Louis d'or or 85 Francs . . . , each payable and deliverable by Miss Ann Davis, living with said testator." Luzzatto had the reputation of being somewhat of a roué.

Aphorisms of Judah Hurwitz, M.D.

The aphorisms of Judah Hurwitz, M.D., are collected in a small, rare volume entitled *Zel ha-Ma'alot** (The Sundial), published in 1764 in Koenigsberg, formerly the capital of East Prussia. The title is apt and pointed, for it delivers what it promises. The expression "sundial" is found in the Bible: "Behold, I will cause the shade of the dial, which is gone down on the sundial of Ahaz, to return backward ten degrees" (Isaiah 38:8). Like the sundial, which reflects the light and shadows of the sun, so do these 365 epigrams in rhymed prose portray the virtues and foibles of human mortals. It is a sort of one-a-day brand of ethical vitamins for the soul, a guide to man toward the correct and straight path.

The author of this small volume, Judah Hurwitz, M.D., was a cultured Russian physician, precursor of the Haskalah movement of enlightenment in Eastern Europe, which took place in the middle of the eighteenth century. At this time there arose in certain Jewish communities a desire to break away from the exclusiveness of Jewish life, to acquire Western culture and be more like their neighbors in matters of language, dress, and habit. Dr. Hurwitz was born in Vilna, a center of Jewish culture. It had a large Jewish population, famous rabbis, scholars, and Hebraists, and several academies. It was at this time that the famous Lithuanian talmudist Elijah ben Solomon (the Vilna Ga-

*This rare book was not in circulation and Professor Harry A. Wolfson made a xerox copy for me. This chapter is dedicated to his beloved memory.
In memory of Prof. Harry A. Wolfson. First published in *New York State Journal of Medicine*, May 1975.

on, 1720–97), lived there, Presumably young Hurwitz had a solid traditional Jewish education, and here in Vilna he continued to study and became well versed in Jewish law and lore, and particularly in medieval Hebrew literature. Like many other Jewish students from all over Europe, his thirst for knowledge took him to the famous University of Padua, where he studied medicine. After graduation he traveled extensively through Europe. In Berlin he became acquainted with Moses Mendelssohn (1729–86), pioneer of German enlightenment. He then settled for a short time in Vilna, where he was appointed physician to the Jewish community. Historians describing the Jewish community of Vilna in that period consider him the foremost intellectual and gifted writer there. He later practiced medicine at Pondeli, Zhagory, and Mitau and finally settled in Grodno. In 1765 he traveled through Germany and went to Amsterdam. He returned to Grodno, spent the remainder of his life there, and died on November 12, 1797. On his tombstone there is an inscription reading "Physician and Philosopher."

Hurwitz was extremely well versed in Hebrew literature and at the same time possessed a wide secular knowledge. He was strongly influenced by Rousseau. His most important work is *Sefer Ammudei Beit Yehudah* (1766), a poetical treatise in which he expounded his moral and philosophic beliefs in the form of a debate. In this work he identified religion with morality. The book includes a poem in praise of him by Herz Wessely and an introduction by Moses Mendelssohn. It also had the approval of many rabbis. His other works are *Sefer Kerem Ein Gedi* (Koenigsberg, 1764), a commentary on Had Gadya, *Gan Eden ha-Ma'ati*, the thirteen articles of belief by Maimonides, *Sefer Maḥberet Ḥayyei ha-Nefesh*, on the immortality of soul (Poreberhye, 1786); and *Sefer Megillat Sedarim*, on the differences between the kabbalists, talmudists, and philosophers (Prague, 1793). In the latter there is a debate among three intellectuals, each one's point of view the product of a different discipline. He also wrote *Heikhal Oneg*, moral sentences (Grodno, 1797) and finally *Zel ha-Ma'alot*.

In *Zel ha-Ma'alot*, a delightful little volume that offers much insight into late-eighteenth-century thought, Hurwitz advocates the humanistic ideals of the Haskalah and criticizes the social conditions of his time. He claims that all but 10 of the 365 epigrams contained in the volume are original. We shall see that some of his ideas were expressed by others in somewhat different form; but just as jewels can be placed in different settings, ornate or simple, these epigrams can be regarded as original. My English translations of selections from *Zel ha-Ma'alot* follow.

> I never saw a jackass with prophetic inspiration,
> Or a mule busy with scientific investigation,
> Or a horse concerned with music appreciation;
> Nor a thickhead go to bed at night,
> Wake up in the morn wise and bright.

Or, as in dictum 87:

> Beware of men who lack reason,
> Run as from a contagious lesion;
> For the latter one may find a cure,
> But there is no remedy for a boor.

Or, proverb 64:

> When your fortune ascends
> All people are your friends;
> But when your luck has gone
> You find yourself quite alone.

The poet Heinrich Heine expressed the same thought in a sarcastic way when he wrote:

> My friends and gnats together
> Have gone with the sunny weather.

Dr. Hurwitz bemoans the brevity and insecurity of human life:

> Wisdom calls—hurry your task every day,
> The Great Reaper may come to take you away.

There is a similar aphorism by Hippocrates—"Life is short, art long, occasion sudden, to make experiments dangerous, judgment difficult"— and Rabbi Tarfon expressed the same thought beautifully: "The day is short and the work is great, and the laborers are sluggish, and the reward is great, and the Master is urgent" (*Avot* 11:20).

But even the short life can be made worthwhile, complete, and full under all circumstances by the pursuit of knowledge. The author exalts wisdom and abhors ignorance.

> Better be intelligent and let life in want pass
> Than a galloping horse or braying jackass;
> The poor may starve for a piece of bread
> While the horse in golden harness clad.

But, he says, to attain scholarship one must start at an early age and continue through his lifetime.

> By beginning to study at an early age,
> In later years one becomes a sage;
> Acquiring the wisdom of generations of yore,
> A fool learning a thousand years knows no more.

To be learned one must not stop learning.

> As long as one searches for the truth,
> He is intelligent and mentally acute.
> Once he assumes he has succeeded,
> Then it seems more wisdom is needed.

Ibn Gabirol expressed this thought in a similar way: "Man is wise only when in search of wisdom; when he imagines he has attained it, he is a fool." Hillel expressed it in his famous maxim: "He who does not increase his knowledge decreases it; one who does not study deserves to die" (*Avot* 1:13).

On the subject of money and its value, Hurwitz knows what it can do, but feels that the pain of not having it is greater than the pleasure of having it.

> There is no virtue in wealth,
> But the lack of it is painfully felt.
> Better to be poor, kind, and hands clean
> Rather than rich, evil, and mean.
> The poor rests in peace without agitation,
> The rich disturbed by his heart's palpitation.

He felt that to be really rich is to be learned, and he is poorest who is ignorant. Learning, unlike wealth, is not inherited; to be educated requires hard study, as he beautifully expresses it:

> Pearls are deep in the sea found,
> Gold is mined from the ground,
> But wisdom lies hidden in books bound.

As a physician and a good psychologist, Hurwitz knew that emotions conquer the will; so he warns in a dictum that one must rule one's life by reason and not by passion:

> He who permits his passion to rule his mind
> Is a fool of the very worst kind;
> During life he is merely a slave,
> In death no peace in the grave.

Or again:

> Man shall ever decide his acts with reason
> Not permit his deeds to make the decision.

He recognizes that emotion impairs the intellect and states in this respect:

> A mind absorbed by passion
> Between true and false finds no discretion,
> Nor differentiate between evil and good
> When one is in an ugly angry mood.

And again:

> Bitter rage and aggravation
> Impair reason and contemplation.

> Aggravation and worry
> are twins by birth;
> Both of them hurry
> Man's return to earth.

Dr. Hurwitz had the delightful gift of coining aphorisms,

proverbs, and epigrams that make very pleasant reading. It is no wonder that this tiny book was published in several editions. His proverbs are homely truths bringing to mind the proverbs of Solomon and the wisdom of Ben Sira. A good name, like learning, is not inherited and must be earned by ethical conduct. His epigrams describing this are picturesque:

> Possessing the escutcheon of morality
> Is better than the earthly pedigree.
> While the noblemen must still good mannered be,
> The good man needs no patent of nobility.

> The noble family tree if of no use
> Who his own name does abuse;
> The noblest pedigree one can claim,
> To have his own a good name.

And, on the rewards of a good name:

> The final goal of all mortals is the same,
> The Simpleton and the Philosopher of fame,
> One the earth covers his worldly shame,
> The other to everlasting life his name.

Dr. Hurwitz, as a good psychologist, has many epigrams revealing his insight. The following is a good example of an analytical psychological projection, the tendency to attribute to another person that which is actually within oneself, and so relieve the ego of guilt feeling.

> If you desire the deeds of others to blame
> Search your own—you will find the same.

Another Hebrew poet, I. L. Gordon, said, "We have bat's eyes for our faults, and eagle's eyes for the faults of others." Hurwitz writes on the subject of time as the great healer and says:

> In good times don't be too gay,
> In evil days do not dismay,
> Like snow in the sun all fade away.

Or, in another:

> A creature is born small in size
> And grows bigger day to day;
> Sorrow like a dark cloud does rise
> But in time diminishes and fades away.

He coined some delightful epigrammatic dictums and proverbs about speech and the use of words:

> Two ears on your head exposed,
> One tongue in the mouth enclosed;
> Hear much—to long speech be not disposed.

> Remember well by the way,
> Guard every word you say,
> Thine tongue may thee slay.

> Beware of the rebel with the smooth tongue;
> Smooth is also the serpents's skin
> To touch—one finds death therein.

> Let thy words flow like a bubbling spring
> For the joy of the one who drinks,
> Not like a stream wherein the bather sinks.

More picturesque is the following adage:

> Wisdom is revealed like the phases of the Moon.
> One phase crescent—dim—another full and bright,
> If it comes like a blast of light
> Like the bat man will take to flight.

Dr. Hurwitz was married to medicine and was busy with his practice, caring for the community of Vilna, but as an ordained rabbi he never lost his love for Hebrew learning and ethics. He coined a number of comely homilies in this area:

> Under a certain condition
> Beautiful is humble submission
> More pleasant to forgive and forget
> Than in ugly revenge a threat.

Worldly pleasures are sweet and good,
But at the end, poisonous like wormwood.

Men prefer innovation
Ever a new sensation
Often abandoning the mighty
For the weak and flighty.

One is born in a world of trouble and prattle
Death is an escape from a constant battle.

Comely silence is the attribute of the humble
But the proud only boast and mumble.

God save us from hearts hard as steel
Souls too weak to feel
Eyes that do not shed a tear
And Ears closed that do not hear.

God turns his ear
To prayer of a broken heart
To an eye that sheds a tear
And troubles that tear one apart.

Silly pride and lust subdue
Humility will appear in comely hue.

When prudence joins a pure heart and clean hand
Then it is dew from heaven on fertilized land.

The noblest kind of deed
Is to help one in dire need.

The world is a stormy sea and very deep
Men on a wiggly bridge in terror creep.

Like a bird is man all his days
Worldly pleasure lays the trap in his ways.

Finally, in a masterful manner, with a few strokes of the pen,
Dr. Hurwitz skillfully analyzes the psychology of the dictator

who assumes absolute power with motives unchecked. In epigram 797 he says:

> Cruelty is the fool's firm stand
> The entire universe his own land
> While the rest of the world go to their end.

The wise physician and philosopher Maimonides had this thought in mind when, in the *Guide to the Perplexed,* he prescribed a remedy for this evil. He says: "It is to our great advantage that the man who knows his station should not imagine that the whole universe exists for him alone."

The Maggid of Dubno:
Fabulous Fabulist

MY FATHER, RABBI ISAAC SAVITSKY

It is written in our sacred lore that no monument need be put up for the righteous, for their own words and deeds serve this purpose: *En osin nefashot la-zaddikim.*

My father of blessed memory built his own monument. Modestly and with true humility, he made the love of the Torah, *Torah lishmah*, "Torah for its own sake," the theme of his life. He made the Torah the measure and standard by which he lived because without this standard, life would have been void and meaningless to him. He strolled daily in the pleasure garden of the Torah and continually found new delights therein. In the field of homiletics, *derash*, he was an expert, and as a partner in his study took in anyone who lent an attentive ear. Many scholarly listeners shared this delight with him in his daily conversations. The Torah was his true spiritual joy, and he regarded himself a partner of all who held this concept. Although he encouraged secular education, he regarded such education as *parpera'ot la-hakhmah*, merely auxiliaries to real knowledge, which is the Torah, and the study of which remained for him always a sacred calling.

He not only preached righteousness, but also by his daily living

Read at the "Amalgamated," Hanukkah, December 14, 1952. First published in *Jewish Forum*, January–February 1953.

endeavored to exemplify true Jewish piety and righteousness.
He loved scholars and was willing to overlook their occasional
shortcomings and would permit no discussion of their human
frailties. He loved the man in every person and searched for the
good in everyone. His life was consecrated to the idea of *Barukh
Mordekhai*, "blessed be Mordecai," i.e., the good that is ever
present in every soul, rather than the concept of *arur Haman*,
"cursed be Haman," or the evil which is latent in the best of us. In
his rabbinic duties, when he delivered eulogies over the departed, he ever guarded against overstatement and exaggeration, but he always found something noble in the humblest of
human beings.

Lehavdil bein hahayyim u-vein hametim, "to differentiate between
the living and the deceased," may I be permitted to say that my
mother has always been his truly blessed companion throughout
his life—a noble soul, a woman of valor, verily an *eshet hayil*, a
beloved wife who, by her consecrated devotion, made possible
the good life he was able to live even under difficult circumstances during the early days when he first arrived in
America. Like his own father of blessed memory, he too died on
Friday, *erev Shabbat*, which according to our tradition is a good
omen and the sign of a *zaddik*, a "truly righteous man." It is,
however, rather symbolic of his entire life, which was a continuous *erev Shabbat*, a preparation for the real Sabbath—the world to
come. He was merely a sojourner in a materialistic world,
gathering spiritual possessions for the real world to come—the
noble deeds by which saintly men build their everlasting
monuments.

*   *   *

Law and lore dominated the spiritual and cultural life of the Jew
for many centuries. On the one hand we have that literature
which is known as the Halakhah, which is the legal interpretation
of the Torah and the continual application of the law to life. On
the other hand, we have that immense literature known as the
Haggadah, which comprises all those matters in talmudic and
rabbinic literature which do not deal directly with the treatment
and exegesis of the law but which are intended to teach and edify
in a general sense. If the Halakhah regulated the life of the Jew

on earth, then the Haggadah brought heaven nearer to him. As a matter of fact, these two tendencies developed concurrently. In the Torah, laws and narratives appeared side by side and together formed the lore. This is equally true of talmudic literature. The Torah is compared to a tree, as it is said, "It is a tree of life to those who hold unto it." If the Torah is a tree, then the Halakhah, the law, is the trunk and the roots, while the Haggadah, the narratives, forms the leaves and fruits. Both of them are essential to Jewish life as the trunk and roots, leaves and fruits are necessary to the compostion of the tree. It is in the shadow of this tree that Jews lived and were protected wherever they went. As a matter of fact, there is no sharp dichotomy between the Halakhah and the Haggadah. In the study of the Torah, one will find poetry in the application of its laws to life and at the same time will discover Jewish laws permeating its legends and narratives.

Now from time immemorial great Jewish scholars and rabbis dealt with the problems of law. They were the great legal minds. Simultaneously, sometimes the very same people also delved into the imaginative or narrative portions of the Torah, the Haggadah. Those who delved into the Haggadah were the popular lecturers to the great masses. Some were itinerant preachers who traveled from place to place expounding those lectures. In some Jewish communities, in addition to a rabbi who was primarily concerned with the law, there was a preacher, or *maggid*, generally known by the name of the city in which he preached. His title was *stadtmaggid*.

One of the most famous of these preachers lived during the eighteenth century. His name was Jacob ben Wolf Kranz, known as the Maggid of Dubno. He was born in the town of Zietil in the province of Vilna about 1741. He died at Zamosc on December 18, 1814. His parables and homely illustrations were very popular. His *meshalim* are still on the lips of many a Jew even at the present time.

The following is a short biography as found in the *Sefer ha-Middot* (Book of ethics) by his disciple Abraham Plahm. Jacob Kranz did not write any books during his lifetime, and all the writings that we have are from his disciples and his son, who published his works after his death as, in reminiscence, in the case of Socrates and Plato.

Jacob Kranz was a descendant of a family of rabbis on both his maternal and paternal sides. He himself was a brilliant student. At the early age of eighteen, he went to the town of Mezhirech, where for two years he occupied the position of preacher. He received six Polish gulden and lodging as salary. Later this was augmented by two gulden. He proceeded successively to Zilkiew, Dubno, Wlodawa, Kalisz, and Zamosc. But it was in Dubno that he remained the longest time, for a period of eighteen years. And it is for this reason that he bears the name "Maggid of Dubno." Later, at the request of Elijah, the Gaon of Vilna, he went to live in that city. The Gaon had shortly before recovered from a serious illness and was unable to study. He sought diversion in the Maggid's conversation.

The following are the contents of the letter sent as an invitation to the Maggid to come to Vilna: "Let me tell you, dear friend, how God in His merciful kindness has performed a miracle with me and restored my health. May I ask you, dear friend, to come to my home as soon as possible to revive my soul, so that the two of us can sit and converse joyfully, etc." The Maggid consented and came to spend some time with the Gaon. As he entered his home, the Rabbi greeted him with, "Well, Reb Jacob, tell me something!.

The preacher replied, again with a *mashal*:

A *melamed* walked ten miles to the marketplace to bring home a goat. Upon arriving home, his wife immediately began to milk the goat but found that she could not draw any milk. The wife began to scream and to scold her husband. Whereupon he answered, "What have you against the poor goat? She is tired and hungry. After such a long journey, let her rest and eat. Then you will milk her."

The rabbi understood the hint and had a table set with food prepared for the Maggid of Dubno.

From his reputation and his works, we can see that Jacob Kranz was an unrivaled preacher possessed of great eloquence. He illustrated his sermons and homilies with parables taken from human life. By the use of such parables he explained the

most difficult passages and cleared up many perplexing questions in rabbinic law. He was such an eloquent speaker, as is told
by his biographer, that he was able to stir his audience, who were
like clay in the hands of a potter. He could make his listeners
laugh or weep.

He once advised some of his colleagues not to listen to him,
telling them they were tender-hearted and he did not wish to
bring them to tears. They laughed and told him not to fear, "We
do not cry easily." They insisted on going, and one eyewitness
tells that no sooner did he begin to talk than a tremor passed over
the audience and his two colleagues were seen shedding tears.
Many rabbinic scholars would consult him on different occasions, regarding him as an authority.

The Maggid of Dubno was a very saintly man who spent most
of his time in study and in prayer. His saintliness is also
well-revealed in the *Sefer ha-Middot*. He was a builder of words,
an architect whose speeches were adorned by various illustrations taken from the life of the Jews of his time. Some orators
impress you as you listen to them, and while they are speaking
you are as though hypnotized, carried away by their gestures or
tone of voice and personality. But their speech loses its fire and
charm when it is reduced to the printed page. The Maggid of
Dubno, however, had more than the gift of a mere orator; for he
left as his heritage an abundance of *meshalim* that still delight the
reader as much as the listener. This is the power of pictures
whether painted on a canvas or merely expressed in words.

The *mashal* is merely an illustration to substantiate or convey
certain truths or ideas. One should not attempt to find flaws in
them, for analogies or allegories are not meant to prove but
merely to illustrate. Like the artistic creation of a painter, the
mashal is not meant to be a perfect photographic reproduction of
an object but rather an impression as seen and felt by the artist
himself. The orator too, in a sense, is an architect and an artist as
well. Some orators build their structure on simple lines, while
others use various decorations to adorn it.

The Maggid of Dubno was a pious and saintly man, as is
revealed in the "Book of Ethics." Again, in preaching about
virtue and sin, he illustrated every topic with a *mashal*. In
speaking of insolence and haughtiness, he says that the insolent

man's ego is very often inflated because of the environment in which he lives. To illustrate this, he gives a very fine example. An innkeeper living in a tiny village used to be consulted by the peasants about the dates of different holidays and the days of the month, etc. His education and authority consisted of his possessing a calendar, which he would consult when the peasants came to him on various occasions to get forecasts of the weather and to ask him for the dates of various fairs and similar questions.

One day the innkeeper said to his wife, "Do you know that I am really a great scholar and I never realized it!" His wife questioned him as to how he had discovered this. He replied that he had heard it said many times that whenever any doubt arose about a date, one went to the innkeeper, who could give the correct answer. The wife was pleased to learn that her husband was such a learned man. Sometime later they had occasion to go to the big city for the High Holidays, and when the innkeeper entered the synagogue, he came in contact with real scholars discussing profound legal matters. He stood amazed, for he could not even understand their language. He finally confided to his wife that he had been mistaken in thinking that he was a great scholar. He lived in a village of illiterate peasants and among them he was a scholar; but when he came to the city and saw the light of the learned, he began to realize that there was not a trace of scholarship in him. He said, "Now I am beginning to realize my position."

In the same book, the Maggid tries to emphasize that the worship of God should be out of love and not out of fear. As a text he uses the phrase, "where the repentant sinners stand, the perfectly righteous are not permitted to stand," and explains psychologically how the repentant sinner attains a greater height than one who has never sinned and was always perfectly righteous and pure. He goes on to explain this further with a typical, homespun tale about a rich man, a *gvir*, who had a servant who served him faithfully.

It happened that there came to the city a rich merchant who, through unfortunate circumstances, had become poor and was in search of a position as an ordinary servant. When the rich man heard about it, he offered to pay him twice the amount that he paid to his present servant.

People asked him why he had done this. His servant had been more than satisfactory, yet now he was willing to pay twice as much to this man. He explained it as follows: "I am aware of the fact that my first servant was very faithful and served me well. But who serves more faithfully than an owner who works for himself! A servant will not burden himself to work more than he is supposed to, or stop to think about the intentions and purposes of his master. If the work becomes too hard and burdensome, he will stop. This is not so in the case of a man who works for himself. His work is always pleasant and delightful; heat and cold or hunger and thirst will not prevent his doing what must be done. That is why I hired this man who once had been wealthy and his own master. He who has worked for himself and then is forced to work for others will do so with the same zest." And when the sinner who all his life was in pursuit of satisfying all his appetites turns all his energies to God, he does so with the same zeal with which he had sinned. So a repentant sinner attains greater heights than the perfectly righteous man.

In explaining the passage in which Joseph said to his brethren: "And now be not grieved nor angry with yourselves that ye sold me hither; for God did send me before you to preserve life" (Genesis 45:5), the Maggid again uses a *mashal*.

A prince had a precious sapphire, but on close inspection he found some defect in it, a scratch or crack in the stone. He consulted many experts and stone-cutters but they all said that if he should try to abolish the flaw, it would only make it worse. Then a wise artisan came along and gave the prince some positive advice. "This stone is very precious, but it will be even more precious if you engrave your name on it with various decorative designs. This design should be carved along the crack, which will then become a part of the engraving. This will make it even more valuable at the end than at the beginning." In other words, the defect led to something that made the stone more valuable and precious; and so the brethren, by selling Joseph, led him to even greater attainments.

Rabbi Kranz, in his fables, used examples taken from life as he knew it. He used the *yeshuvnik,* or "village man": the merchant, the rich man, the poor man, and in a great many of his fables, he also used the physician. In the following pages I have selected a number of fables, or *meshalim,* in which a physician plays the leading role. They reveal how well the maggid understood the

function and psychology of the physician as well as the mind of
the patient who comes under his care. These are not only
delightful but also very instructive.

It is said in the *Ethics of the Fathers:* "For perforce thou wast
formed and perforce thou wast born, and perforce thou livest
and thou wilt die, and perforce thou wilt in the future have to
give account and reckoning before the Supreme King of Kings,
the Holy One, blessed be He." The question was raised, if a man
is born against his will, lives against his will, and dies against his
will, why should he have to account for all his deeds? The
Maggid of Dubno explained it by the following *mashal.*

There was a rich man who was the father of two daughters; one was
unattractive almost to the point of repulsion, while the other was the
hysterical, screaming type. But it so happened that they met their
suitable mates. The ugly daughter married a man who was blind, while
the other, who had always been screaming her head off, married a man
who was deaf. They lived happily in spite of their defects.

Sometime later a famous physician came to town and offered to cure
the bridegrooms of their serious defects by surgery. The doctor, with
his skill, restored hearing to the one and sight to the other; but lo and
behold! When one opened his eyes and saw his wife, his life became
very unpleasant, to say the least, while the other found that he was
almost driven to madness by hearing for the first time the hysterical
screaming of his wife. Because of their unhappiness, which began with
the successful operations, they refused to pay the agreed-upon fee.

They all went to the rabbi for his advice and judgment. The
defendants claimed that they were worse off now than before the
operations, whereupon the physician replied, "If you want, I can
restore you both to your former conditions. I can perform another
operation on each of you so that *you* will be blind and (pointing to the
other) *you* will be deaf." They both refused this offer! Therefore the
rabbi declared that the physician was entitled to his fee.

And so this *mashal* explains that even though a man is born
against his will, he does not want to die. Hence, he must pay the
consequences and account for all his deeds.

In explaining the passage in Exodus in which Moses uttered
the command to appoint judges in every village, town, and city,
the Maggid asks the question, "Would people think, because
they needed so many judges and officers in all the towns and

villages while other people got along without them in certain districts, that crime is prevalent among the Jews?" In the following *mashal* the Maggid seems to have a deep understanding of the real function of the physician as well as that of the officers and guardians of the law. He tells of a man of the East who asked of a German, "Tell me, why do you have a doctor in every little town and village, while we have one only in our great cities, and yet we do not have many sick people? And when I talk with the Germans, it seems that everyone has a complaint in spite of all your doctors. We neither have as many complaints nor do we go to a doctor unless we are really seriously ill."

The German replied, "I shall tell you the difference. You do not call a doctor unless you are about to die. We have periodic examinations, and we are told how to prevent becoming ill as much as we can."

The same is true about courts of justice; we have judges and teachers of the law in every location, so as to guide us from getting into more serious trouble.

In explaining the passage in Exodus, "This is in the first month of the year . . ." the Mishnah says that the Holy One is called the first, Zion is called the first, Esau is called first, when they come to build the Temple, that is called first, and Esau will be punished in the first month.

This is like unto two beggars who were wandering from city to city to collect alms. One was strong and healthy and had no ailment, while the other beggar was just the opposite. From his head to his toes he was one mass of complaints. The healthy one used to insult and ridicule him and at the same time, boast of his perfect health. So the poor, sick beggar would weep quietly to himself, praying to the Lord to help him not only from his illnesses but also from the insults and taunts of his ignoble partner. God listened to his prayers.

They came to the capital and heard that the strongest man in the kingdom had died, one who had been the pride of his king and court. At the same time, the most famous physician of the land also had died. The king desired two men who could fill the vacancies caused by the deaths of his two famous subjects. His soldiers went out in search of such men. After searching for some time, his soldiers found two eligible men. The king was very pleased but wanted proof as to whether they were as great as the men whose places they were to take. The strong man, the giant, said, "Bring before me the strongest man and with one touch of my finger, I shall knock him down." The physician then said, "Bring before me the most complicated and difficult case, and I shall cure the patient." And so the king commanded his servants to carry out this experiment.

Messengers were sent everywhere to bring two such people before the king. They came upon the two beggars, placed them in a carriage, and brought them before the king. The healthy beggar boasted as usual, "It is only because of me that you too are brought before the king." The sick beggar silently poured out his heart to God, without uttering a word. The healthy man was brought before the king together with the strong man who was about to display his unusual strength. With one touch, he was brought down and the strong man proved his claim and won the title. Then the sick beggar was placed under the care of the physician and was cured of all his aches and pains.

There are some who boast of their strength and power as if there were no God or judgment; but soon each one will receive his reward, for it is the divine power to lower the mighty and raise the downfallen. The proud and mighty nations shall be humbled, while the small and weak nations will be exalted. Did we not see an example of this during the last war, when the world of the boasting Fascists and Nazis was shattered, while the tiny nation of Israel has risen to new glory!

In explaining the text in Isaiah (33:1):

> Woe to thee that spoilest, and
> thou wast not spoiled;
> And dealest treacherously, and
> they dealt not treacherously with thee!
> When thou hast ceased to spoil,
> thou shalt be spoiled;
> And when thou art weary with
> dealing treacherously, they shall
> deal treacherously with thee,

the Maggid of Dubno employs a fact used in medicine:

It is a general rule, when a patient demands treatment from a doctor, that very frequently he has to suffer the unpleasantness of treatment. It is sometimes necessary for a doctor to remove the damaged limbs, decayed bones, rotted flesh, and consequently the patient suffers. If the doctor has at some time in his life suffered as a patient himself, thus knowing the pain of illness, he will be able to sympathize with the patient who trembles and shrieks with pain, and he will recall how he too has suffered, and he will believe the patient and have compassion and will sympathize with him and go slowly and lightly. But the doctor who is healthy in body, and was never affected by disease, will find it hard to believe the patient, and when the patient screams in agony, he may even laugh or be angry or indifferent, and this will hurt the patient even more.

This is said similarly about Nebuchadnezzar. You did the spoiling but you were never spoiled. Therefore you will never feel the suffering of the people under you. You will laugh at them.

How well Rabbi Kranz understood the psychology of the patient.

It is said in the Talmud that when the Jews said, "Let us send someone to spy on the land," the Holy One, blessed be He, said, "I shall not prevent them, but I swear that they will never enter." The question was asked, how can He swear for the outcome when man has freedom of choice? Perhaps they might even praise the land, thus being worthy to enter. Rabbi Kranz again explains it with a *mashal*.

It is like unto a man who, on having a gastrointestinal disturbance, called in a wise and famous physician. The doctor examined him and told him to have no fear. He said, "I had a similar case and now the man is perfectly well, but in order to cure you, I must give you an intoxicating drink, and then, while you are sleeping, I shall be able to do whatever I have to do." The patient asked, "What will you do to me then?" The physician replied, "It is not necessary for you to know." Whereupon the man stated, "Well, then I shall have to go to your former patient and find out what you are going to do to me." The physician answered, "If you do not believe that I can cure you, I swear that you will die as a result of this illness." And with that the physician went away angry. Later, people asked the doctor, "How did you know that he would die?" He replied, "When this man, who has no confidence in me, goes to my other patient to whom I gave the sleeping potion, after which I opened his abdomen and rearranged all the things, and hears what has to be done, then he will refuse the treatment and will therefore die."

And so it was in Palestine that there were giants and brave men; but if God fights on the Jews' side, then they will be able to overcome them. But one must believe in all of God's miracles and promises to be

brought to the land of milk and honey. If the Jews sent spies to the land
and saw the giants, their hands would weaken. Man has freedom of
choice, but the omniscient God knows the results.

The following *mashal*, or example, conveys the concept of
psychosomatic medicine in the simplest words, yet more clearly
than could be done in psychological terminology. It reveals the
greatness and the deep understanding of this preacher, how well
he understood the human mind and how profound simple
thoughts may be. In commenting on Leviticus 15, "This is the
law of the leper," the *Midrash Rabbah* says: There is a story of a
peddler who, selling his wares in the nearby city of Sepphoris
would shout, "Who wants to buy the elixir of life?" One day, as
Rabbi Yannai was sitting in his home, he heard the peddler's cry.
He called him over and said, "Come here and let me have some
of this elixir of life." The peddler replied unto him, "You and
men like you do not need it." But the rabbi imposed on him and
finally the peddler, taking the Book of Proverbs, read, "He who
desireth life guard thy tongue from evil." Rabbi Yannai said,
"King Solomon too proclaimed the same thing: 'He who guardeth his mouth and tongue guardeth himself from trouble.' "
Then the rabbi added, "All my life I read these quotations and I
never understood their meaning until the peddler came and
made it clear to me."

The preacher of Dubno asks the proverbial question, "What
new revelation did Rabbi Yannai find in the simple verse, 'He
who desireth life guard thy tongue from evil'?" For, after all, the
peddler merely pointed out that sentence without any commentaries. And he answers:

It is like a patient who is confined to a sickbed with a disease of the chest
or lungs. When the doctor visits and thoroughly examines him, he
warns him that he must not get angry, he must not be aggressive, nor
avaricious for money or glory. He adds that if he should find that he
does not earn much from his business while his neighbor profits a great
deal, he must not take it to heart. He tells him not to be envious or
jealous of anyone and to keep away from lust. Now, if a fool were
listening to the doctor's advice, he would be amazed and say, "What
business is it of the doctor, whose main function is to treat the body, to
tell his patient not to be angry, not to worry or get excited? This is in the

domain of preachers, whose business it is to preach morals, such as temperance, etc. Why choose to tell him these things at this particular moment, when the man is seriously ill?"

The really wise man will understand that the doctor is right. It is not because of fear of the Lord that he commands the man to guard himself from evil traits. Rather it is to cure him physically; not to prepare him for the world to come, but rather to rid him of his bodily ills in this world. For all these evil traits shorten the life of man upon the earth and bring upon him all kinds of disease. Evil traits corrupt the blood and bring disease, and lead man quickly to an untimely death. It is for this reason that the doctor warned the patient against these evil characteristics. This is the story of the peddler that is told in the Midrash. Like numerous peddlers going from town to town selling medicine, he shouted to all that he had the elixir of life, not as a preparation for the future world, but very simply as a medicine that would prolong man's life on earth. This medicine was peace, equanimity, freedom from falsehood and the evil traits that cause anger and heartache. He who is careful will lead a peaceful life, while the reverse is true for those who do not heed this advice.

Summary

In this paper an attempt is made to describe the distinguished preacher of the eighteenth century, Rabbi Kranz, the Maggid of Dubno. There were many preachers of this kind, though not so famous, who led a saintly life and preached Jewish ethics and morals to the Jewish people. They accomplished much more than was done by the popular Jewish lectures. They were doctors to the Jewish soul and spirit. What other entertainment did the Jews possess behind the locked walls of the ghetto but to go in the afternoons, especially on Saturdays, to listen to a delightful preacher expound Jewish law and lore? While they listened, they were actually entertained and amused. At the same time, the instruction was like a flavored syrup that contains the ingredients of a medicine. Each one of the sermons and fables expressed delightfully and vividly, like a skillful illustration, the contents of the Book of Books. Instead of a brush and canvas, the preachers used words and painted pictures on the minds of their listeners.

Here was a man who had a vivid imagination. He felt and lived the Jewish life and tried to convey it to his listeners. He was a good psychologist, for he knew how to attract his audience and keep their attention. He also revealed another attribute. He was a born teacher who knew how to keep the attention of his pupils and, at the same time, convey his ideas to them. Such a man was the Maggid of Dubno.

Each preacher had his own peculiar sing-song style of preaching. The men would sit and swallow his words like little birds who open their mouths in anticipation when their mother brings them food.

The Maggid would usually conclude with the following words: *Uva le-Ziyyon go'el,* "May a redeemer come to Zion soon, especially in our own days, and let us say amen!" As a matter of fact, it is the preacher who helped to keep up the hope of the Jews in spite of all catastrophes while waiting for the Messiah. He awakened the dormant spirit in Jews and kept alive the Messianic hope of his people. From this type of preacher finally came the national orator, men like Masliansky, Shmarya Levin, Barondess, and others, until we finally reached the goal in the establishment of the State of Israel.

Dr. Joseph Chasanowich

The Jewish people are designated as *Am ha-Sefer,* a people of the book, not only because they gave *the* Book—the Bible—to the world, but also because of their intrinsic love and devotion to books in general. When Israel was forced to leave his native land, he took the book into exile together with his wandering cane. The dedication of the Jews to this concept is evident in the number of Jewish laws regarding books. For example, if a book should fall down, one is to pick it up and kiss it. Torn and damaged volumes are not merely discarded; they are to be buried with dignity in the cemetery. The joy of possessing books and the pleasure of the reader is revealed by the ethical will of the physician and Hebrew translator from Arabic into Hebrew, Judah ibn Tibbon (1120–1190). He wrote, "Make your books your companions; let your cases and your shelves be your pleasure grounds and orchards. Bask in their paradise, gather their fruit, pluck their roses, take their spice."

In modern times one who deserves an honored place for his noble, almost lifelong effort to establish a Hebrew library in Jerusalem is the pioneer Zionist and bibliophile, Dr. Joseph Chasanowich. He was born in Gontonetz, government of Grodno, Russia, on October 22, 1844, son of Aaron Chasanowich. His mother died during his childhood, and he was brought up by his grandfather. He received the traditional Jewish education in the Hebrew school and had secular studies at the gymnasium of Grodno.

First published in *Rhode Island Journal of Medicine,* March 1974.

After completing his studies there, Chasanowich went to Germany and studied medicine in Koenigsberg. While still a student he became a volunteer assistant surgeon to one of the military hospitals of Berlin during the Franco-Prussian War (1870–71). He received his M.D. degree from the University of Koenigsberg in 1872. Returning to Russia, he pursued his studies for the State Board at Dorpat and began to practice in Bialystok. He served for several years as the physician to the Jewish hospital, where he worked most of his life, devoting particular attention to the poor. There he founded the Lerrotti ha-Zedek Hospital Society, and he also founded the Hovevei Zion Society for the education of Jewish youth in the spirit of Zionism. He served as president of this society for many years, and during this whole period took an active part in the Zionist movement.

At the beginning of World War I, Chasanowich went to Central Russia to the city of Yekaterinoslav to treat the war refugees. In 1883 he set out to settle in Eretz Israel (the Land of Israel), but was forced back because of a cholera epidemic. In 1884 he was a delegate to the first Conference of the Hovevei Zion (Lovers of Zion) in Kattowitz. Later he became one of the fervent disciples of Theodor Herzl, the founder of Zionism. In 1894 he visited Palestine, and while there conceived the idea of founding, together with the order of B'nai B'rith, a Hebrew National Library in Jerusalem; but his plan was necessarily postponed because unfortunately he aroused the displeasure of the government.

Soon after his return to Bialystok, Chasanowich was involved in a situation in which an anti-Semitic Polish physician in that city was accused of malpractice in regard to a Jewish boy. So vehement was Chasanowich's defense of the victim that he was forced by the government to leave the town for a period of two years. (Russian injustice to Jews has a long history.) During this period he established himself at Lodz, but in 1893 he returned to Bialystok and began to formulate his plan for the future.

Chasanowich dedicated much of his time to the collection of ancient and rare books for the National Library in Jerusalem. It is said that in his medical practice he made no charge to the poor, and that if he visited such a family owning a rare book, he would acquire the volume and pay for it. Toward the end of his life he published leaflets urging Jews to donate books, writing at one time, "In our holy city of Jerusalem, all the books written in Hebrew, and all books in all languages which deal with the Jews and their Torah; all the writings and drawings dealing with their life—will be treasured." He published similar announcements in the Jewish magazines and papers in Hebrew and in other languages. His vision was realized when the National Library was first built on Mount Scopus in Jerusalem and later at the new university campus at Givat Ram outside the city. Altogether he collected 63,000 volumes, 20,000 of them in Hebrew and some very rare. These books each have a bookplate reading *Ginzei Yosef* ("Joseph's Treasures").

Chasanowich was a man who gave everything he had, of his time and of himself, to a noble cause, until in 1915 he was forced to move to Yekaterinoslav, where he died in poverty in the old people's home in 1919.

There are people who live to satisfy the wishes of their ego without concern for others, and there are those more noble, whose superego reigns supreme; this controls man's primitive impulses and allows him to dedicate his life to the well-being and happiness of others. Such a person was Dr. Joseph Chasanowich, a bibliophile who considered books the treasure-house of the wisdom of generations. He decided to collect books for a National Library in Jerusalem so that the generations to come might draw from these fountains of wisdom.

Francis Weld Peabody

Scion of a learned family, Francis Weld Peabody, with inherent noble traits, was a great physician and teacher by the grace of God. Religion and Bible permeated the home in which he was brought up. Both his grandfather (Ephraim Peabody) and his father (Francis Greenwood Peabody) were Unitarian ministers. From 1881 to 1914 his father was a professor at Harvard University. Francis Greenwood Peabody was the author of *Reminiscences of Present-Day Saints,* published in 1927. His son indeed had many of the characteristics and traits of a "modern saint" in medicine.

Born in Cambridge, Massachusetts in 1881, Francis Weld Peabody entered Harvard College in 1900 and graduated in three years, receiving his degree *cum laude* at commencement in 1903. In 1907 he received his medical degree from Harvard Medical School. While he was a student there, Dr. Reginald Fitz, who was the first to diagnose appendicitis, detected in him the potentialities of a great physician, and he suggested to young Peabody the possibility of a career, which at that time was hardly practicable, in academic medicine.

During the next few years Peabody followed the route which would qualify him for that position. He interned at the Massachusetts General Hospital from 1907 to 1908 and was an assistant resident physician at Johns Hopkins Hospital from 1908 to 1909. He was a fellow in pathology at Johns Hopkins Hospital from 1909 to 1910 and was a student of chemistry at the

First published in *Medical Way,* April 1952.

University of Berlin in 1910. From 1911 to 1912 he was assistant resident physician at the hospital of the Rockefeller Institute, and he was a resident physician at the Peter Bent Brigham Hospital from 1913 to 1915. In 1917 he was a member of the Red Cross Commission to Rumania. He was assistant professor of medicine at Harvard Medical School from 1915 to 1920 and professor of medicine at Harvard Medical School from 1921 to 1927.

Although he died at the age of forty-six, Dr. Peabody succeeded in crowding his years with many fruitful endeavors. A bibliography of his works indicates a list of no less than sixty-nine publications, most of them dealing with fundamental problems in the field of internal medicine. Some of the general articles with regard to the practice of medicine will remain forever as inspirations and guides to physicians; for example, his paper "Care of the Patient" (*Journal of the American Medical Association,* 1927). It is in this paper that he reveals the noble traits of a great physician. Every patient was to him an individual, a personality, and not merely a case labeled under a certain category of disease. This is what he tried to instill in his students and colleagues. He was ever kind and never too busy to listen even to undergraduates. He encouraged them in their endeavors. The following episode reveals the ideal teacher: It was my privilege to study medicine under Dr. Peabody and as a student of his I gave him a reprint of a paper on the "Jew in Medicine." After reading it, he sat down and wrote me a letter in the following words:

My dear Mr. Savitz:

Thank you very much for the reprint of your article on the "Jew in Medicine." I have read it with much interest and I think it shows very clearly what I have never entirely understood, namely, why so many Jews enter the medical profession. This tendency is, as you suggest, unquestionably inherited and medicine is by inheritance one of the legitimate outlets of the intellectual activities of the Jews.

With all good wishes,
Francis W. Peabody

He never permitted a student, in presenting a case, to say,

"This is case number so-and-so." Dr. Peabody would say, "This is not just a case with a number; he is a person who has a name and should be treated as a personality and not as a case with a number."

Dr. Peabody diagnosed his own ailment as a malignancy; he knew that his days were numbered and yet he refused to give up. He wanted to die teaching, conveying knowledge and inspiring students so that they might carry on his ideals of the noble profession of medicine. He loved the students, and they in turn admired him. Those who had the privilege to come in contact with this man will ever cherish his memory.

Not only did he try to convey to his students the fundamentals and principles of medicine, but even the slightest details were not neglected so as to produce the ideal physician. At one time, in his section, a patient had a deep abscess, and Dr. Peabody asked, "How do you treat such a condition?" One of his students replied, "By poulticing." Dr. Peabody then asked, "How do you prepare a poultice?" The student did not know, and Dr. Peabody told him that the next morning at seven o'clock he should come up when the nurse was preparing a poultice and watch her do it; he would be a better physician for that.

Another of the students fell ill with pneumonia. Dr. Peabody took care of him, and when the student was better, he turned to him and said, "Now that you have had the disease you will be a better physician, and you will understand better the patient who suffers from such an ailment." Those were the kind words of encouragement of this great physician and teacher.

He was always kind and just in his criticism; ever ready to encourage and give credit where credit was due as well as to correct when the student was in error. In his sections each of the students was required to write a paper on some medical topic and summarize the literature pertaining to it. One of his students selected cardiospasm, which was not on the list of subjects to be chosen. When the student told Dr. Peabody of his idea, his reply was, "By all means do it!" and then he proceeded to give him a list of men who had written on that subject, for Dr. Peabody was thoroughly acquainted with the literature of internal medicine. The student summarized the literature, the treatment consisted of passing bougis and dilating the cardiac sphincter. The student suggested that before starting such crude treatment the patient should be examined for a possible mental complex which might produce this symptom. Since this was in 1924, before psychosomatic medicine was born, the student's assistants were gloating, for they felt that this undergraduate who dared to go into untrodden paths would surely receive the scorn of the teacher, as they probably would have done, but instead Professor Peabody turned to the student, to the amazement of his assistants, and said, "I am inclined to agree with you, and there is such a patient on the ward. I want you to cooperate with the resident-in-charge and see what you can find." Such were the ever-encouraging words of that great teacher in whom every student found a loyal friend and guide.

I wish to conclude with a sonnet written by Dr. Peabody's father on the untimely death of his beloved son.

F.W.P.

In full midsummer of maturing powers,
His wisdom ripening for its harvest-tide,
Exploring subtle truths in tireless hours,
Unscathed by selfishness, unspoiled by pride,
Serene as if composed to quiet sleep,
He greeted death and calmly smiled on pain,
Content if other laborers might reap
Along the whitening furrows of his grain.
"What blindfold fate, with cruel irony,
Devises such irreparable harm;
Bids the unfit survive, and ruthlessly
Effaces learning, leadership, and charm?"
So, while the light of faith was hid by tears,
And the dear life escaped our tardy praise,
We marked the unripe grain of waiting years,
And mourned the wastage of the unlived days.
Yet who shall set a term of fruitfulness,
Or reckon life by years of gain or loss?
Did not the Master of the soul confess
His work was finished when He bore His cross?
Was death at thirty an untimely end,
Or have the ages found His words untrue—
"Into Thy hands, my Father, I commend
The perfect work Thou gavest me to do"?

Ah, not in tasks fulfilled, beloved son,
But in the way made plain, the lives renewed,
The healing touch, the long research begun,
Was your sufficient source of quietude.
To cheer and reassure the suffering,
Desiring life, but unafraid to die;
Where is, O Death, for such a soul thy sting?
O Grave, how barren is thy victory!

Hirsch Loeb Gordon, M.D.

Dr. Hirsch Leob Gordon was a versatile scholar who mastered several disciplines of learning, as evidenced by the number of academic degrees that adorn his name like medals on the lapel of a famous general. He was a prolific writer and the author of several books. He was skilled in several languages, including English, Hebrew, Yiddish, and Italian.

Hirsch Gordon was born on November 26, 1896 in Vilna, Russia—the Jerusalem of Lithuania—a dynamic Jewish cultural center. His father, Elijah Gordon, was a profound scholar who wrote four books dealing with homiletics and legalism, then became rabbi of the city, and later in the United States. In his youth Hirsch received the traditional Jewish education in the elementary Hebrew school—the *heder* and continued his studies in the famous rabbinical seminaries of Slobodka, Lyda, and Volozhin. These were the nurseries of many erudite Hebrew scholars who later accepted chairs of learning in the outstanding universities of the United States.

In 1914 Hirsch Gordon was graduated from the Institute of Jewish Learning in Odessa. It is related that as a student in Odessa he suffered great poverty, but his lack of sustenance was compensated for by the friendship of the famous Hebrew poet laureate, Ḥayyim N. Bialik, who at that time lectured at the

First published in *Rhode Island Journal of Medicine,* July 1975.

Institute. Gordon was entranced by Bialik and absorbed every word while taking notes. The poet befriended his admirer, and their friendship flourished.

Gordon reported the contents of the lectures to the Hebrew daily, *Ha-Zefirah,* and in return received fan letters from the editor, Nahum Sokolow. For lack of funds Gordon lived in a poor neighborhood in a miserable dwelling. On one occasion he heard a knock on the door and asked in Russian, "Who is there?" "I am Sokolow," was the answer, "and I am looking for Mr. Gordon." Ashamed of his poor abode, Gordon replied, "Mr. Gordon does not live here."

In 1910, at the age of fourteen, Gordon entered the famous rabbinical seminary (*yeshivah*) at Volozhin, a great center of talmudic learning. Students came from everywhere to study there, but the mere study of the Talmud and its commentaries and complexities did not satisfy Hirsch Gordon. His thirst for knowledge led him secretly to read many secular books, magazines, and articles in the Russian language. He was particularly attracted to Leo Tolstoy's works. Quietly he pursued his secular studies and prepared himself to enter the Russian gymnasium (secondary school). At the same time he was busy with other activities, including Zionist fund-raising groups. Under the pseudonym of "Gil" he published an article in *Ha-Zeman,* a Hebrew daily, on the status of education in the Volozhin *yeshivah.*

Gordon came to the United States in 1915 and became a citizen in 1922. Here in the land of freedom and opportunity he toiled in several fields of learning, mastered several disciplines, and succeeded in accumulating more academic degrees. He was a perpetual student, and his thirst for knowledge had no limit. In 1922 he received a Ph.D. degree in Semitics from Yale University; he also studied medical history there under Castiglioni.

In 1923 Gordon received an M.A. degree in international law at American University, a Doctor of Humanities in Egyptology at Catholic University, and in 1926 an M.A. in psychology at Teachers College of Columbia University. He received his M.D. degree at the University of Rome in 1934, and also a Doctor of Letters in classical archaeology from the same university. He was a diplomate of the Institute of Legal Medicine in Rome and a

Doctor of Hebrew Studies in Talmud from the Jewish Theological Seminary in New York in 1938.

Not satisfied with one profession, Hirsch Gordon wanted to absorb and embrace several, like a bee that flies from flower to flower to produced honey. His abundant learning bore fruit, and he became a prolific writer. He was the author of many literary and scientific articles as well as several books. Included among his writings were a book on shock therapy, an article on the basilica and the stoa, and a paper which detailed psychological concepts in the Bible, Talmud, and Zohar. He translated from the Arabic a medieval work by Moses Maimonides titled *The Preservation of Youth*. He published an article in Hebrew on "Autopsies According to Jewish Law," including a historical review of postmortem examinations.

But Gordon's *magnum opus* was a book titled *The Maggid of Caro* (New York: Pardes Publishing Co., 1949). Here is how it came about. On January 31, 1942 Gordon read a paper on "The *Maggid* of Caro" before the Hebrew-speaking Medical Society of New York City. It was discussed by Professor I. S. Wechsler of Columbia University and Professor Arturo Castiglioni of Yale University. Dr. Gordon, believing that the topic of *maggidim** would prove to be of interest to students of psychology and psychiatry, expanded his paper into a book. The book is the story of Joseph Caro (1488–1575), who was an eminent talmudic scholar and codifier of rabbinic law. Born in Toledo, Spain, he was exiled with his family in 1492. After much wandering they settled in Safed, Palestine, where Joseph later founded a *yeshivah* (Hebrew academy) and wrote his code *Beit Yosef* (The House of Joseph) and its classical abbreviation, the *Shulḥan Arukh* (The Prepared Table).

The *Shulḥan Arukh* was a collection of the views of previous codifiers and Caro's decisions on disputed points. Caro was interested in Kabbalah—mysticism—and was greatly influenced by it, so much so that he claimed that religious secrets were revealed to him by an angel (the *maggid*). There are a number of comments in the books about the *maggid*. The scientist Albert Einstein had a logical explanation of revelations of this type. He

---

*Heavenly spirits or agents. *Maggid* is the singular.

felt that a new idea comes suddenly in a rather intense way—intuition is nothing more than the outcome of accumulated earlier intellectual experience.

As a physician Gordon had his own explanation of Rabbi Caro:

It was his ambition to become that supreme authority—to become president of that seat of learning. To justify his wish, high appraisal of his person rose to the surface of his consciousness. To be sure, such pretensions on the part of Caro were not crowded with the halo of ordinary modesty. But while a great man may affect outward humility and meek behavior, he cannot silence within his soul the triumphant voice of his true eminence and power.

How true psychologically—as is illustrated by the arrogant man who ever boasts of his humility.

Gordon led a full and active life professionally. He attended the Neurological Clinic of Mount Sinai Hospital of New York beginning in 1935, and later also at Maimonides Hospital in Brooklyn, the Pilgrim State Hospital in Brentwood, Long Island, and the Bellevue and Kings County Hospitals in New York and Brooklyn.

In World War II he served as a major in the Army Medical Corps and was chief of shock therapy at the Veterans Administration Hospital in Northport, New York. In 1947 he became chief neuropsychiatrist for the Veterans Administration at Jacksonville, Florida, and later was neuropsychiatric consultant to the Surgeon General of the Army. This was followed by duty in the Public Health Service as senior surgeon, and then as chief of neuropsychiatry at the Marine Hospital on Staten Island. In 1951 he became a member of the Board of Appeals for the New York State Selective Service.

Dr. Gordon was a fellow of the American Geriatric Society of the American Psychiatric Association, and of the American College of Physicians, and was a member of the New York Academy of Medicine. In 1967 he received the Maimonides Award given by the Michael Reese Hospital and the College of Jewish Studies, both of Chicago (awarded to a physician chosen either from this country or from abroad who has contributed substantially to both medicine and Judaica). In 1968 he received the American University Alumni Award.

Summary

Dr. Hirsch Loeb Gordon was a versatile scholar, psychiatrist, historian, author, and journalist, proficient in English, Hebrew, Yiddish, and Italian. He was the recipient of degrees in several disciplines and made noteworthy contributions to each of them.

PART II
Geriatric Studies

Geriatric Axioms, Aphorisms, and Proverbs

The axiom is an established and universally accepted principle or rule. An aphorism is a terse saying embodying a general truth. For example, the aphorisms of Hippocrates define the symptoms of disease. The characteristic of an aphorism seems to be the disproportion between the simplicity of the expression and the richness of the sentiment conveyed by it. The proverb, on the other hand, is more complex and has more intense meaning and greater specific gravity. It is a saying which is frequently repeated, forcibly expressing some practical truth as the result of experience or observation. It is usually uttered by some wise man and adapted by the public. "It is one man's wit and many men's wisdom." Like good wine, it is more esteemed with age. Ibn Ezra said, "An epigram is a beautiful meaning expressed in a few clear words." He described the anatomy of the proverb: "A proverb has three characteristics: a few words, right sense, fine image. But above all it must contain a message." It is to our advantage to be acquainted with the proverbs and sayings of the wise. As Ben Sira warned us, "Despise not the discourses of the wise, but acquaint yourself with their proverbs." Israeli said: "The wisdom of the wise and the experience of ages may be preserved by quotations."

First published in *Journal of the American Geriatrics Society*, 1968.

Our lives are enriched by learning the proverbs of all ages. Proverbs may or may not have a rhyme, but they always have a good thought. Proverbs are useful tools of writers and orators. They make writing more picturesque and catch the eye of the reader. Words of the orator reverberate in the ears of the listeners. Because of their high specific gravity, proverbs are economical; they convey many ideas with a minimum of words. When the rabbis of the Talmud wanted to convey the idea that a reasoning mind is worth more than learning, they expressed it in a brief proverb: "One grain of pepper is worth more than a basketful of pumpkins." Or, when a certain rabbi was accused of following an atheist, he excused himself by saying proverbially that when he found a pomegranate, he ate the inside and threw away the shell.

Since a proverb is "the wit of one man and the wisdom of many," it is sometimes difficult to identify the author of a wise saying. It becomes common property, to be used by any intelligent person. The only proverbs we recognize are those from the Bible, particularly the Book of Proverbs; many a thirsty one drinks from this fountain.

The following is a collection of axioms, aphorisms, and proverbs dealing with old age in its several manifestations— physical, mental, and therapeutic. They were selected from various reading materials. An attempt was made to group them as far as possible in the divisions: longevity, the characteristics of old people, age in contrast to youth, physical and mental states, therapeutics, and miscellaneous sayings.

AXIOMS, APHORISMS, AND PROVERBS CONCERNING OLD AGE

He is old who acquires wisdom.

Talmud

There are old men at sixty and young men at ninety.

A man is as old as he's feeling,
A woman is as old as she looks.

Mortimer Collens (1827–1876)

Life is long if you know how to use it.

Seneca

He lives long that lives well, and time misspent is not lived, but lost.

Fuller

Many old people, their age hardly seems to belong to them at all.

Those keep long youngest who love most.

Age and youth look upon life from the opposite ends of a telescope; it is exceedingly long . . . it is exceedingly short . . .

Beecher

We reap in old age what we have sowed in our earlier years.

If you must be a dear old lady at seventy, you must begin early, say at about seventeen.

Agnes Moude Rayden

Age is an opportunity no less than youth, than youth itself in another dress.

Longfellow

Age is a woman's hell.

If you wish good advice, consult an old man.

English Proverb

The age at which one shares everything is generally the age when one has nothing.

Youth is a blinder, manhood a struggle, old age a regret.

Benjamin Disraeli

Youth—a boon appreciated in old age.

Milestone—may become millstone.

Age I do abhor thee, youth I do adore thee.

Shakespeare

Life which we find too short, is made up of many days which we found too long.

Old age—one foot in the grave.

Three score summers, when they are gone, will appear as short as one.

Whenever a man's friends begin to compliment him about looking young, he may be sure they think he is growing old.

Washington Irving

Age is the most terrible misfortune that can happen to any man; other evils will mend, this is every day getting worse.

A mature person has a sense of balance in all things, is judicious, slow to condemn and to praise.

The art of life is to pass gracefully from childhood to maturity, from youth to old age, and last, as Montaigne said, "To learn to die."

Old people's behaviorisms are usually an exaggeration of their earlier traits.

Old age merely releases the brakes.

Many an old man makes up for certain technical deficiencies by greater serenity, wisdom, and judgment.

Gray hairs are death's blossoms.

Never too old to learn.

Learning makes a man fit company for himself.

Old age is honorable.

Old be or young die.

If you would not live to be old, you must be hanged when you are young.

Everyone complains of his memory but nobody of his judgment.

A man not old, but mellow like good wine.

Ulysses

Older and wiser,
I love everything that is old;
Old friends, old times, old manners,
Old books, old wines.

You cannot avoid old age.

Old bees yield no honey.

Old dogs do not bark for nothing.

Old socks want much patching.

Of young men die many,
Of old men escape not any.

Old men go to death, but death comes to a young man.

The old man's staff is the rapper at death's door.

They who would be young when they are old must be old when they are young.

To the old, of a molehill he makes a mountain.

The young man knows the rules, but the old man knows the exceptions.

Oliver Wendell Holmes

The superior man blames himself,
The inferior man blames others.

None so old than he who hopes for a year of life.

An old man is a bed full of bones.

Save something for the man that rides the white horse—old age.

Use legs and have legs.

Young men think old men fools, and old men know young men to be so.

The glory of young men is their strength, and the beauty of old men is the hoary head.

Proverbs 20:29

Scholars, as they grow older their wisdom increases.

Talmud

The illiterates, as they grow older their minds become confused; but not so with the scholars, the older they grow, their minds become clearer.

Talmud

Elisha ben Avuyah said, "If one learns as a child, what is it like? Like ink written on clean paper. If one learns as an old man, what is it like? Like ink written on blotted paper."

Sayings of the Fathers

Rabbi Yose ben Judah of Kfar Babli said, "He who learns from the young, what is he like? Like one who eats unripe grapes, or who drinks wine from a vat. And he who learns from the old, what is he like? Like one who eats ripe grapes or drinks old wine."

Sayings of the Fathers

Rabbi Meir said: "Look not at the flask, but at what it contains; there may be a new flask full of old wine, and an old flask that has not even new wine in it."

Sayings of the Fathers

Rabbi Eleazsar ha-Kappar said, "Envy, desire, and ambition drive a man out of the world."

Sayings of the Fathers

The shock of retirement is not that you stop doing something, but that you do not start doing something else.

Most patients are not afraid of death but are reluctant to die.

It is notorious that the desire to live increases as life itself shortens.

Ramon y Cajal

Crabbed age and youth cannot live together
Youth is full of pleasure, age is full of care.

Shakespeare

Not by years but by disposition is wisdom acquired.

Plautus

He who is of a calm and happy nature will hardly feel the pressure of old age.

Plato

Wrinkles if due to age are fine; if due to habit, they are coarse. The former appear late; the latter may begin in early life.

Investigate thoroughly all complaints, minor as well as major, of the aged.

It is rare for a geriatric patient to have only one complaint, it is rare for him to have only one diagnosis.

A good rule of geriatric care is that no patient shall be nursed in bed if this care could possibly be avoided.

Not all confusion in the aged is due to mental deterioration.

Bromides in elderly patients provide symptoms indistinguishable from a true psychosis.

Nothing hastens old age more than idleness.

Idleness and the bed are the two pallbearers of the living aged.

Association with the young is the best antidote to burdensome aged.

The aged are always lonesome.

Milk is the best food for the aged as for the young.

Fasting is a wonderfully effective medicine for many an ill.

The shedding of teeth may be the natural safeguard for the aged against overeating.

Sir Henry Holland

More numerous are those killed by the pot than those killed by starvation.

Shabbat 135)

A person's general adjustment to aging is profoundly affected by his feeling about age.

Some at seventy can exercise more strenuously than others at forty.

Old age does not create new habits; it only deepens old ones.

Diet in old age is like that in the young.

Every man desires to live long; but no man would be old.

Pope

Typical temperature curves such as are found in typhoid fever and malaria are rare in the aged.

A recurrence of early tuberculosis is mild; a primary infection in old age is fatal.

Neither pulse, pain, nor temperature is a reliable guide in determining the diagnosis in the aged.

Stimulation of a degenerating organ or tissue hastens the degeneration.

Some are aged before they are old, some are old but not aged. Geriatrics deals with the senile state, not with years of life.

I. L. Nascher

The saddest thing about old age is that its future is behind it.

Ramon y Cajal

And they die an equal death, the idler and the man of mighty deeds.

Homer

What will cure a young person may kill an old one.

Death is Nature's device for securing abundant life.

Goethe

Life is growth, the retardation of growth is old age, and its cessation is death.

Many grow old before they arrive at age.

Sir Thomas Browne

When a man is old he must do more than when he is young.

Goethe

The high prize of life, the crowning fortune of a man, is to be born with a bias to some pursuit, which finds him employment and happiness.

Emerson

Years following years steal something every day; at last they steal us from ourselves away.

Pope

Old age must learn neither to withdraw nor to impose oneself too much.

The aged should be treated as a personality, not as an object of management.

Patients who have a devoted family seldom seek entrance into a home for the aged.

Old age gives good advice when it is no longer able to give a bad example.

Old age is a tyrant which forbids the pleasures of youth on pain of death.

Few people know how to be old.

In maturity nature cures, in senility nature kills. Aid nature in maturity, prevent death in senility.

I. L. Nascher

The senile stoop, due to anatomical changes, comes on slowly and late; the senile slouch, due to psychic causes, comes on early and rapidly.

The mind occupied with some task does not dwell upon self and death.

The aged often deny pain to avoid examination.

It is not every patient who is fit to be told the truth about his disease.

A sane mind consists in a good digestion of experience.

Clifford Allbutt

As land is improved by sowing it with various seeds, so is the mind by exercising it with different studies.

Pliny

In order to improve the mind, we ought less to learn than to contemplate.

Descartes

The best physicians are Dr. Diet, Dr. Quiet, and Dr. Merryman.

Dean Swift

It takes sixty-five muscles of the face to produce a frown and only fourteen muscles to produce a smile.

Wine and wisdom improve with age.

S. Rubin

Nobody grows old by merely living a number of years. People grow old only by deserting their ideals.

S. Ullman

Man is always trying to make something for himself rather than something of himself.

What is the worst of woes that wait an age?
What stamps the wrinkles deeper on the brow?
To view each loved one blotted from life's page
And be alone on earth, as I am now.

Lord Byron

Youth is a blunder, Manhood a struggle, Old Age a regret.

Disraeli

Your old men shall dream dreams, your young men shall see visions.

Bible (Proverbs)

If you gather not in youth, how will you find in old age?

Apocrypha

Youth is a garland of roses; old age a crown of willows.

Talmud

What a man does in youth darkens his face in old age.

Talmud

Youth is fair, a graceful stag,
Leaping, playing in the park.
Age is gray, a toothless hag,
Stumbling in the dark.

Peretz

There is nothing more enviable than to have an old head and a young heart.

Sanders

You are as young as your faith, as old as your doubt; as young as your self-confidence, as old as your fear; as young as your hope, as old as your despair.

S. Ullman

The hoary head is a crown of glory.

Bible (Proverbs)

With the ancient is wisdom and in length of days understanding.

Bible (Job)

Dishonor not the old; we shall all be numbered among them.

Apocrypha

Honorable old age is not marked by length of time . . . but understanding is gray hairs . . . and an unspotted life is ripe old age.

Apocrypha

Gauge a country's prosperity by its treatment of the aged.

Nathan Bratzlav

Geriatrics in Biblical and Talmudic Literature

There are several terms in Hebrew designating the declining years of life. The Hebrew word for "old man" is *zaken,* which is connected with the word *zakan,* meaning "beard"—the most striking sign of old age. Then there is the term *sevah yamim,* which means "saturated with days." Another phrase, *kabir yamin,* means "rich in years." In the Mishnah, the age of sixty is called *ziknah,* and the age of seventy is called *sevah.* In the Bible we find a definite statement with regard to the age of man, "The days of our years are threescore years and ten: and if by reason of strength they be fourscore years, yet is their strength labor and sorrow" (Psalms 90:10). In the Talmud, too, it is stated if one dies at eighty, he has reached old age (*Bava Batra* 75).

The ages of man is a favorite theme of all moralists and is treated in the Mishnah in the following manner: Man's life is divided into three periods—preparation for life till twenty, activity from twenty to sixty, and decline from sixty onward.

At five years the age is reached for the study of the Scripture, at ten for the study of the Mishnah, at thirteen for the fulfillment of the commandments, at fifteen for the study of the Talmud, at eighteen for marriage, at twenty for seeking a livelihood, at thirty for entering into one's full strength, at forty for understanding, at fifty for counsel, at sixty a man attains old age, at seventy the hoary head, at eighty the gift

First published in *Journal of the American Geriatrics Society,* 1965.

of special strength, at ninety he bends beneath the weight of years, at a hundred he is as if he were already dead and had passed away from the world. (*Avot* 5:24)

The aged were greatly respected by the Jews. The origin of this attitude may be found in the commandment, "Honor thy father and thy mother: that thy days may be long upon the land which the Lord thy God giveth thee" (Exodus 20:12). There are various commentaries explaining the meaning of the reward given for respecting one's parents, "that thy days may be long upon the land." No reward is mentioned for keeping the other commandments. It seems to me that the most simple meaning is, if you honor your father and mother and let them live to ripe old age, your children in turn will respect you and you will get your reward during your life. This brings to mind the famous folk story of an old man who used to break the dishes while eating. So his son carved wooden dishes for him. One day the son found his little boy, the grandchild, carving, and he asked him, "What are you doing?" The child replied, "I am making a spoon for you, father, for when you are old." There is a definite commandment in the Bible which states, "Thou shalt rise before the hoary head and honor the face of the old man" (Leviticus 19:32). As a matter of fact, the word *zaken* is the Hebrew acronym of "He who acquires wisdom." But it is wisdom acquired by learning; gray hair is no guarantee that there is profound intellect in the gray matter, nor is youth synonymous with ignorance. This was well described by one rabbi in the following simile: Rabbi Meir said, "Look not at the flask, but what it contains. There may be a new flask full of old wine and an old flask that has not even any wine in it" (*Avot* 4:27). In other words, the age of a person or of a teacher is no criterion of the soundness and value of his scholarship; unripeness of judgment is not the exclusive possession of the young, nor is wisdom of the old. The aged were consulted on every important occasion. As it is written in the Midrash, the people of Israel are compared to a bird. "Just as the bird is unable to fly without wings, so are the people of Israel unable to do anything without the help of their elders."

Experience alone is not sufficient. It is the acquired learning that is emphasized. As one rabbi said, "Where there is no wisdom, there is no old age" (*Berakhot* 39). Another said, "Scholars, the older they get, the wisdom is increased; while the ignorant, the older they get, the more silliness is added" (*Shabbat* 152). The sages realized very well the physical frailties and failings of old age. As one put it, "The stones that we set upon in our youth have declared war on us in our old age." The minutest obstacle disturbs the old man. As they expressed it, "To an old man even a small mound appears to him as the highest mountain."

In the Talmud, too, there is an anecdote which describes symbolically the advancing years of old age (*Shabbat* 152a). A rabbi was asked why he had not met the emperor in a certain place, and he pleaded old age in the following words: "The mountain is snow, and it is surrounded by ice, the dog does not bark and the grinders do not grind." The declining years of life are described in Ecclesiastes 12:3–7 as follows:

3. In the day when the keepers of the house shall tremble,
   And the strong men shall bow themselves,
   And the grinders cease because they are few,
   And those that look out shall be darkened in the windows,

4. And the doors shall be shut in the street,
   When the sound of the grinding is low;
   And one shall start up at the voice of a bird,
   And all the daughters of music shall be brought low:

5. Also when they shall be afraid of that which is high,
   And terrors shall be in the way;
   And the almond tree shall blossom,
   And the grasshopper shall drag itself along,
   And the caperberry shall fail;
   Because man goeth to his long home,
   And the mourners go about the streets:

6. Before the silver cord is snapped asunder,
   And the golden bowl is shattered,
   And the pitcher is broken at the fountain,
   And the wheel falleth shattered into the pit;

7. And the dust returneth to the earth as it was,
   And the spirit returneth unto God who gave it.

According to the Talmud, the keepers of the house in verse 3 are the flanks and ribs, the strong men are the legs which support the body but grow bent in old age, the "grinders" are the teeth, and "those that look out" are the eyes. The verse presents a picture of the terrifying effect produced upon the members of the household by a storm. The keepers of the house are the staff of servants, and the strong men are those appointed to guard the buildings against robbers.

In verse 4 "the doors shall be shut" alludes to the apertures of the body; "the sound of the grinding is low" means the failing power of the stomach to digest food; "one shall start up at the voice of a bird" indicates that even a bird will awake him from sleep; "the daughters of music shall be brought low" means that even the voices of male and female singers sound to him like a whisper because of deafness. Another explanation is that an old man has little sleep at night and awakens as soon as the birds begin to sing. "The daughters of music" is probably an idiomatic expression for "musical notes" which are brought low, i.e., sound softer than they really are to an old person with impaired hearing.

In verse 5 "they are afraid of that which is high" can be interpreted as meaning that a small knoll looks to the old man like the highest of mountains when he has to walk up it; "terrors shall be in the way" means that when he walks on a road his heart is filled with fears because his legs are unsteady; "the caperberry shall fail" refers to the lack of effect of this fruit which excites sensual passion (Talmud); and many interpret "the almond tree" as depicting the whiteness of the hair.

The rabbis of old realized the difficulties of the aged in acquiring new knowledge. As one puts it, "If one learns as a child, what is it like? Like ink written on new paper. If one learns as an old man, what is it like? Like ink written on blotted paper" (*Avot* 4:25). In other words, in youth, the mind is like new paper; whatever is written on it remains clearly legible. So the mind of youth is similarly fresh to receive impressions and new instruction. In old age, however, new learning leaves a blurred impression on the mind.

On the other hand, it is more advisable to receive instruction from mature and older people than from the young. As one rabbi put it, "He who learns from the young, what is he like? Like one who eats unripe grapes or drinks wine from the vat. And he who learns from the old, what is he like? Like one who eats ripe grapes or drinks old wine" (*Avot* 4:25). Knowledge received from youth is immature; it is like unripe grapes which set the teeth on edge and wine from the vats which is not matured and leads to intoxication. Similarly, teaching by the young leaves a great deal to be desired. But instruction by the elders is like old wine, which is a source of health and festive joy. So is ripe knowledge which only the experience of years can supply.

There are other aphorisms in the Talmud comparing youth and old age.

Rabbi Yose ben Kisma said: "Two are better than three, and woe for the one thing that goes and does not return. What is that?" Said Rabbi Ḥisda: "One's youth." When Rabbi Dimi came, he said: "Youth is a crown of roses; old age is a crown of willowrods." It was taught in Rabbi Meir's name: "Chew well with your teeth, and you will find it in your steps, as it is said, for then we had plenty of victuals, and were well, and saw no evil." Samuel said to Rav Judah: "O keen scholar! open your mouth and let your food enter. Until the age of forty food is more beneficial; thenceforth drink is more beneficial."

That the child is the father of the man is beautifully expressed in the words of the Talmud, "Things one does in his youth often blacken the face in his old age" (*Shabbat* 152). Or, in other words, "Happy is one's youth that does not bring shame in his old age" (*Sukkah* 91). This is equally true of the physical condition as well as the spiritual life, as is well expressed in the following: "The warm baths that his mother gave him in his youth and the oil that she anointed him with served him well in his declining years" (*Ḥullin* 24:2).

The gray hair of old age is a crown of glory if one ages naturally, with grace, but in some instances the frailties of old age will overtake a man prematurely. This is well portrayed in a homily in the Midrash on a verse in the Bible: "Then Abraham gave up the ghost, and died in a good old age, an old man, and full of years" (Genesis 25:8)—interpreted as "A man may be old but is not full of days, and there is one whose life is full of days and he is not old." In other words, the chronological age does not always correspond with one's actual condition. The life of a man is like a book, and if there are years without active life, it is like a book containing many blank pages.

The frailties of old age will often overtake a man prematurely because of fear due to the aggravation of children, a wicked wife, or the mental tension of war.

The sages made a keen observation with regard to children. "Sometimes a son will feed his father pheasant, the choice meat of the feathered birds, yet drive him from this world, and the son will inherit purgatory. Another son will burden his father yet he will inherit the rewards of the future world" (*Kiddushin* 31).

Comment

There are crystalline insights and profound observations in the Bible and the Talmud with regard to old age and the aged. Love of children and respect for the aged are the two criteria by which the civilization of a people is measured. In primitive times, infanticide was common. Children were offered as sacrifices and the aged were liquidated. As the Midrash tells, in the city of Luz in Palestine, "When men became old they were taken out and left outside of the walls of the city to die." The Bible warns against the offering of children as sacrifices, as illustrated in Genesis in the story of the contemplated sacrifice of Isaac. According to Bible records, not only were the aged preserved and guarded, but they occupied a prominent place in the social and political system, and in private life were respected as the repositories of knowledge.

Mental Hygiene for the Aged

It is the tragedy of man that he begins to look with disdain on old age as he himself gets along in years. Everyone wishes to live long, but no one wants to be old. Man laments the brevity of life, but when he achieves longevity he is not content with his hoary age. The psalmist describes the problem of old age as follows:

The days of our years are threescore years and ten, Or even by reason of strength, fourscore years; yet is their pride but travail and vanity; for it is speedily gone, and we fly away. (Psalm 90:10)

Historic Views on Old Age

The Greek tragic poet Euripides, who lived from 490 to 406 B.C.E., complained, "Youth is always dear to me; old age is a load that lies more heavily on the head than the rocks of Elma." Sophocles, too, lamented, "All evils are ingrained in long old age; lost wits, unprofiting actions, empty thoughts." Yet he lived actively to ninety and Plato to sixty-two, both busy and creatively productive to the end. Men used to fear death, but in the present era they seemingly have adjusted themselves to the unavoidable end, but worry about incapacitating old age. The geriatrician constantly hears, "I do not fear death, but I do not wish to grow old and suffer."

There is a Yiddish gibe based on the Hebrew word for "old

First published in *New York State Journal of Medicine*, October 1976.

age," *ziknah,* ironically abbreviated to read *ziphzen,* which means "sighing," *krechzen,* which means "groaning," *nissen,* which means "sneezing," and *husten,* which means "coughing." This represents a most pessimistic view of old age, but there is a more logical and optimistic way of evaluating man's advancing years. When the bright summer and all of its accompanying joys are gone, we do not bemoan the oncoming winter with its cold and snowy winds, but rather we don suitable clothing and make further preparations so that we may find new pleasures in the coming season. Man's life is a continuous process of adjustment to new situations and to new stages of life as they arise. Each season has its advantages and its disadvantages; we do not bathe in the ocean in winter, nor do we ski in summer. We manage to accommodate ourselves to the changing conditions and seek to appreciate every opportunity for our benefit and enjoyment. In the fall we "winterize" ourselves and our equipment so that we may be comfortable and able to enjoy the new season with its own special pleasures. Every stage of life has its benefits and its trials, and as one gets on in years he must "olderize" himself, to use a new term, to meet the new situations he will face in this period of his life. For this stage of life can bring many joys and much satisfaction, and it can be filled with meaning.

To be sure, there is vigor, freshness, and strength in youth, but old age has many compensations. As the wise men have said: "The glory of young men is their strength; and the beauty of old man is the hoary head" (Proverbs 20:29).

As the years advance, maturity and judgment increase as a result of the lessons learned in life's school of experience. As man's age increases, he finds the exceptions to the rules and laws youth absorbs from books. The old man need not despair if the years have wrinkled his face and diminished his vigor and his strength; he can exult in the realization that his inner self is capable of continued growth. With the maturity of age comes more tolerance and keener judgment as well as fewer illusions and superstitions. There comes increased spiritual strength to compensate for the loss of physical vigor. He can continue his growth in those areas where ideas become more valuable than material possessions. While youth worships the body, old age can find value in the spirit, and this becomes a way of life; an aged person becomes a mature man and not an old man. If the mind expands with these spiritual treasures, a source of enjoyment in themselves, a beneficial effect is produced on the physical body, and this may actually prolong useful life.

The anecdotes which follow illustrate well these statements. Solomon, in his Book of Proverbs, taught: "The hoary head is a crown of glory. It is found in the way of righteousness" (Proverbs 10:30). Hence, various rabbis who had attained an advanced age were asked by their pupils as to the probable cause of their attainment of that mark of divine favor. Rabbi Hehumah answered that in regard to himself, God had taken cognizance of three principles by which he had endeavored to guide his conduct. First, he had never striven to exalt his own standing by demeaning his neighbor; second, he had never gone to his night's rest harboring ill will toward his fellow man; and third, he was not penurious. The last of these qualities is well illlustrated by the Hebrew word meaning "to give," *natan,* which is a palindrome and can be read backward as well as forward; for those who give, more is given to them.

Another rabbi replied that he believed himself to have been blessed with a long life because, in his official capacity, he had invariably set his face against accepting presents, mindful of Solomon's writings, in which he said, "He that hateth gifts will live" (Proverbs 15:27).

It is interesting to note that the rabbis of the Talmud, who scrutinized every word in the Bible and whose analytic minds searched critically for the latent meanings in its laws, also investigated the prelude to longevity. It was not mere curiosity, but rather an attempt to investigate its etiology. As a result of these searchings, they developed a number of psychomatic aids aimed at prolonging the span of life. This is illustrated in a tale in which a rabbi asked Rabbi Joshua ben Korha, "By virtue of what, have you reached such a good old age?" Rabbi Joshua answered him, "Do you begrudge me my life?" The questioning rabbi replied, "This is a point of Torah and it is important for me to learn." Since it was for the purpose of study and not idle curiosity, he was answered thus: "Never in my life have I gazed at the countenance of a wicked man" (*Megilah* 28a). Now this may be construed as meaning that Rabbi Joshua saw only the good in every face, for each person has a bit of the angel and a bit of the demon in him. And when Rabbi Zera was asked by one of his disciples, "By virtue of what have you reached such a good old age?" he replied, "Never in my life have I been harsh with my household, nor have I stepped in front of one greater than myself, nor have I gone four cubits without Torah, nor have I rejoiced in the downfall of my fellow (men), nor have I called my fellow by his nickname" (*Megillah* 28a). All of these virtues enumerated by the scholarly rabbis of old may not always lead to a long life, but they help one to a meaningful life. Verily did the wise Ecclesiastes say, "The words of the wise are like goads" (Ecclesiastes 12:10); whereas a goad directs the heifer to plow in the furrow it is meant to plow, so do the words of the wise direct a man in the right way. It is the humane virtues that lubricate the wheels of life; they banish grief and sorrow and make life more pleasant and so prolong life itself.

One such noble trait is humility, that rare quality of retaining a modest sense of one's own merit. Such a person is content to accept himself for what he is and does not dissipate his energies lamenting his failure to achieve the high places for which he lacks qualification. If one admits the superiority of a greater personality, there is more merit in accepting the situation than in trying to cast doubt on the greatness of the other.

There is in every human being the desire to be a somebody, and it is better to strive to be the best somebody one can be than to waste time and effort in the attempt to be somebody else. Happy is the man who dares to be what he is. One of the greatest somebodies in history, the redeemer of his people, a lawgiver, and the father of civil liberty for all humanity, as well as the father of preventive medicine, was Moses. The Bible describes him in very few words; "The man Moses was very meek" (Numbers 12:30). This great man of whom the poet Heine wrote, "How small Sinai appears when Moses stands upon it," lived to the age of 120 years, creative and modest throughout.

Problems of Aging

The complaints, resentments, and discontents of the aged are many, but on analysis many are not so dark as they are painted, nor are they all to man's disadvantage. The most frequent and general lament is that of weakness. Gone is the vigor, freshness, and enthusiasm of youth. To be sure, youth is a race, and old age is a walk. As the years go on time becomes shorter, and the distances become longer; one's pace is slower, and this is Nature's way of prolonging life. One can often cover greater distances at a slower pace, sometimes overreaching the runner. As the Russian proverb puts it, the slower you ride the further you travel. Experience may have taught a great many shortcuts that will compensate for the lack of speed.

Another common complaint of the aged is the loss of memory. It is a well-known adage that old age is the mother of forgetfulness. This too can be considered an advantage in some respects, for man would indeed find it hard to live on if all the unhappy and unfavorable experiences of the past were to be clearly preserved in his mind. Just as the patient who has recovered from a critical illness forgets the frightening details, so must old age bury its dead past and involve itself in the pleasures that added years can bring. To be practical, if there are important details and facts which one really wishes to retain, these can be recorded in a small notebook; the actual writing down helps to impress the fact on one's mind, and then you have your memory in your pocket.

Most of the special facilities connected with bodily organs do lose their acuity in the advancing years, such as the faculty of hearing by which sound is perceived. We frequently hear the aged complain that their hearing is not what it used to be; this is quite correct. However, "hard of hearing" of the aged in many cases is partly due to "hard of listening" because the elderly have a tendency to be extremely loquacious. They narrate endlessly about their youthful pursuits and accomplishments, but they are not so generous in listening to the chattering of others. I would suggest to the mature elderly person that he lend his ears to his neighbor's tales as his neighbor does to his.

Among the host of woes of the aged is the lament that as they get older they are subject to numerous illnesses. Of even greater concern is the fact that they look on old age itself as a disease. This is not so, no more than that infancy or adolescence in themselves are diseases. During the early years the young are subject to a number of children's diseases before they build up the bodily defenses of immunity. The functioning of the human body is miraculous in itself; the physiologic function of the little finger is more complicated than any elaborate machine. So it is but natural that something in this complicated structure goes wrong occasionally, and the longer we live the greater the chances for malfunction in one organ or another. But it is for this reason that we have medicines and physicians to administer them. I would urge the elderly to discuss their ailments with their physicians in the consulting room, and not to bewail their problems to friends or neighbors. As the wise Ben Sira wrote: "Honor thy physician according to thy need of him with the honor due unto him; for verily the Lord hath created him" (Ecclesiasticus 38:1).

We find that many aged persons grumble about minor discomforts which, when put in proper perspective, may be considered an advantage. The entire gastrointestinal tract is one hole of blame. First and foremost is the ever-present murmur of poor appetite, for which there is a demand for a variety of tonics. As a rule, the aged person eats more than he should, which is another preoccupation, and consumes more calories than his daily requirement. Little do the aged realize that the poor appetite is Nature's safeguard for the preservation of health. More people die from feast than from fast, and as it has been said, "A healthy young man with poor appetite will preserve health and add years to his life." What we now diagnose as an acute heart attack, or myocardial infarction, was often called acute indigestion at the beginning of this century because it frequently occurred after heavy meals which triggered the attack. Indulgence in food was recognized many years ago as being injurious to health and to the shortening of life. The following anecdote in the Talmud reveals this concern:

Alexander asked the Elders of the South what a man should do to live. They replied, "Let him kill himself (doing good)." He then asked them what a man should do to kill himself. They replied, "Let him live" (in self-indulgence). (*Tamid* 32a)

Another source of the aged person's constant complaint is the problem of too much leisure time, and the dissastisfactions arising from this seem to be his major preoccupation. If some of this leisure time were devoted to concentration on a productive hobby, a great many symptoms of illness would vanish. This is the period in one's life when one can and should develop new and absorbing hobbies or further develop past interests for which there was not sufficient time in the busier years. A psychological definition of interest is background, and as knowledge of a subject increases so does interest. This interest may be compared to the structure of an edifice; the higher it rises the deeper must be the foundation.

Dealing with Old Age

To live is to act; to do something that absorbs your mind and makes good use of your time, the most valuable treasure of added years, makes for an exciting existence. To be idle is to live in a vacuum, and this is detrimental to good health. Someone has said that an idle man is like a dead person, except that he occupies more space. Work is a source of joy to the mind and therapy for the body. Men, as a rule, are unnerved and worried when they are faced with retirement, not so much from the prospective loss of their positions as at the prospect of nothing to occupy their time. Just as one plans financially for retirement, it is equally important to fill the leisure time which will come. This makes for purpose in life and provides the happiness and contentment which one derives from doing something well that he enjoys doing. There are many skills that can be learned or further developed in the later years. The old proverb that you cannot teach an old dog new tricks is a lazy man's alibi; it is but a pretext to explain idleness. It is the rationalization of the idler, and the proverb has been somewhat modified to state that if the teacher knows more than the dog and the dog is willing to learn, the dog can be taught new tricks. It is literally never too late to learn. It is true that it make take the aged person longer to learn, but that which is lost in time is often gained in depth. The older person, with his past experience, sees much between the lines that is invisible to youth. When the elderly person continues the pursuit of knowledge he is doubly rewarded: first by the new knowledge which enriches his life by its actual possession, and second, by the therapy of the mental activity.

Most geriatricians find that the edlerly patient often experiences the feeling of loneliness. The late poet Robert Frost describes sensitively and accurately the loneliness of old age in his poem "An Old Man's Winter Night." The first line sets a mood, "All out-of-doors looked darkly at home," and the poet continues:

> A light he was to no-one but himself
> Where now he sat, concerned with
> A quiet light, and then not even that.

Loneliness may not be a total disadvantage, but like salt, a little is good and a lot undesirable. To be alone at times provides an escape from tumult and allows for contemplation. Some of the most profound thoughts are developed when one is alone and undisturbed. Too much time alone sometimes brings on depression, but there are many remedies to be suggested. A man need never be lonely in the company of books, and like the manna that fell from the heavens there are books for everyone according to his taste and mood. The hotel guest who finds a Bible when he enters his room experiences a greeting as from an old friend. Furthermore, just as a daily walk helps to preserve the physical vigor of the body, a stroll through the garden of literature keeps the mind active and alert. The old English adage that says, "Use your legs and you will have legs," may be adapted to the mind. The Talmud states this well: "The illiterates, as they grow older, find their minds confused; but not so with the scholars—the older they grow the clearer their minds become."

It is understandable that the older person experiences the loneliness and melancholy that comes when his friends pass on, one by one. As Lord Byron wrote:

> What is the worst of woes that wait on age?
> What stamps the wrinkle deeper on the brow?
> To view each loved one blotted from life's page,
> And be alone on earth, as I am now.

This is truly a most distressing experience. But one must hold on to remaining friends, and at the same time, endeavor to enter into new relationships. True friends are the nearest relatives;

stated by the wise man, "But there is a friend that sticketh closer than a brother" (Proverbs 12:24). Good friends increase your joys and share your sorrows; a friend is the impregnable citadel of refuge in the state of existence. But, as is well known, one must give of himself to have a friend, and it is interesting in this connection to note that the Hebrew word for "friend" is *dod*, another palindrome that can be read in either direction.

Another antidote against loneliness was wisely prescribed by an old Hebrew sage, Hillel, during the first century B.C.E. He is the author of the golden rule, "Do not do unto others that which you would not have them do unto you" (*Shabbat* 31a). He authored another golden rule to forestall loneliness: "Separate not thyself from the community" (*Avot* 2:5). In other words, identify your individual life with that of the community in which you live, and do not stay apart from it. Take advantage of its facilities and programs, and share in its weal and woe. The new associations made in these programs and causes bring stimulus to the mind, activity to the body, and relief from loneliness.

In summary, I would suggest that the elderly must realize that life is a continuous process of adaptation to its many stages. Each period of life has its advantages, it special joys, and its disadvantages and problems. As one lives on to a relatively long life, there are features which seem unpleasant, such as the lined face, the gray hair or lack of hair, and feet that are slow to run. Man must make a conscious effort to avoid boredom and the feeling of uselessness by utilizing his accumulated experience and wisdom. As we grow more mature, we become more tolerant and perceive the latent qualities, as well as the defects, in people, and we do not expect perfection. Diamonds, even with slight imperfections, are still precious stones. In a sense, life at this period becomes more vivid and more of a challenge. I suggest the following decalogue for the aged.

1. You are a man grown in years and in maturity, and not just an old man.
2. Do not worship youth as an idol, for it is only a period of life and it is not all golden.
3. Do not complain in vain of old age; the only way to avoid it is to die young.

4. Remember the seventh decade—six decades shalt thou work and on the seventh thou shalt rest; but have an avocation.

5. Honor and rejoice in thy gray hair so that you will experience the promise in Robert Browning's poem, "The best is yet to be."

6. Do not kill time recounting what you were and where you went; rather be concerned with what to do and where you are going.

7. Act your age—do not undertake the unmanageable tasks when your face is lined with fatigue.

8. Do not steal years from your life by wasting precious time.

9. Do not fail to recognize and value the advantages and opportunities of old age.

10. Do not covet youth once it is gone.

Humanizing Institutional Care for the Aged

*Thou shalt rise up before the hoary head, and honor the
face of the old man.*—Leviticus 19:32

Modern medicine has succeeded in prolonging the life-span of
the individual. Each day more than 1,000 persons reach the age
of sixty-five, and while the population of the United States has
doubled since 1900, the number of persons sixty-five and over
has more than quadrupled. It is predicted that by 1975 one in ten
of our population will be in this upper age bracket. We have
made great advances in making people older, but we have done
little to give meaning and fullness to those added years. We find
ourself in a situation similar to that of the possession of the
atomic bomb. Science has been able to release the tremendous
nuclear energy of the atom, but it has not been able to teach us
its wisest use, and such is the fate of the longer life-span. Are
these added years to mean more time to live or merely more time
to die?

Added to this situation is the fact of the gradual disintegration
of the cohesive family unit, in which parents formerly occupied
the center of the family circle. Gone is the "father image" to be

First published in *Journal of the American Geriatrics Society,* 1967.

125

admired and emulated. Instead we find parents being gradually pushed to the periphery, and frequently cast away as if by centrifugal force. Since they cannot live with their families, they are placed in institutions. They are, to be sure, provided with board and room, but this is not what the aged desire or deserve, and it is not at all surprising that they rebel, consciously or unconsciously. The biblical poetical adage, "Man does not live by bread alone," is for the aged person a truism and very real, since what he longs for most of all is the preservation, respect, and dignity of his personality—his capital *I*. He resents being a number, even in a most luxurious palace. From our intensive work with the aged, we have found that the best and most natural place for an older person is his own home and his own environment. If this is not possible, conditions most nearly approximating his own home should be provided for him.

Provisions for the Comfort and Safety of Residents

How can this be accomplished in an institution that cares for the aged? How can we create that psychological and social environment most suitable to the older person and make him feel that it is his home? Soldiers, dressed in uniform and crowded into barracks, are pressed to submerge their individual personalities, to become a number in a company which can act as a unit; and this is essential in a military force. An institution for the care of the aged should represent the reverse of this policy. Everything possible should be done to preserve and respect the personality of the individual. We must rid ourselves of our "edifice complex," building massive structures with decorative fronts, which often result in striking architectural achievements but do not necessarily make a "home" for the aged person. The emphasis in an institution for the aged should be on building from the inside out, to make a place where one can find small units to create a more homelike atmosphere. The buildings should not be in an isolated area, and should be neither like a "leper colony" nor like a lush vacation resort built for people who wish to escape from the hustle and bustle of the city. As a matter of fact, older people prefer a location in a populated area—one in which young and middle-aged people reside, in addition to the elders of the community. They do not like to be surrounded entirely by old people; they ignore their own gray hair and old age. An eighty-six-year-old resident said, when asked how he felt, "How can you feel well when you are completely surrounded by old men?"

We must revamp our attitude toward old age. We are living in a youth-oriented age, with the emphasis on doing everything possible for youth. We seem to have gradually abandoned the commandment "honor thy father and thy mother" and to have substituted "love thy child and thy little brother." We find established chairs in pediatrics in our medical schools and countless psychologists and researchers studying the emotions and the mind of the child. We do not find similar chairs in geriatrics. Many hours of instruction are spent on the preparation of formulae for infants from birth to six weeks, and then to six months, and so on, but little time is spent on a formula for making the years after the sixth decade more meaningful and satisfying. We should learn to look at things through the eyes of our older men and women. We should change our philosophy and rid ourselves of the prevalent misconceptions of old age and the undercurrent of prejudice toward old people.

While youth is admired, respected, and encouraged at all times, many times old age is looked upon as a hopeless, chronic ailment to be gotten over with, like the measles. Old age is no disease; neither is it synonymous with chronicity and hopelessness. It is the autumn period in human life, and it can have the beauty of a fall season. The aged, like people in other age groups, have personalities and sensitivities and want to be loved; they, too, form complexes when ignored and neglected.

Though the aged have lost their vigor and the strength of their youth, they have, on the other hand, accumulated a great deal of wisdom and experience in the school of life. History records that many nations, in time of need and stress, have called upon old people to come to the rescue. During the last war the free world was saved by old men. Wisdom is often more valuable and precious than mere strength and vigor. If our attitude changes, the entire problem of the aged will take on a new look.

With this concept in mind, the practical solutions for the care of the aged will fall into a new pattern. Their homes will not consist of huge buildings of the "skyscraper" type, but rather will have a master-plan to coordinate a number of smaller units grouped harmoniously for their various purposes. There will be many more accommodations for one person in a single room where no one will intrude upon the privacy of the individual, and the aged person will feel that he still has a little corner that belongs to him alone. Married couples will have accommodations that will permit them to live together in this autumn period of their lives. In institutions, where double rooms predominate, the most common ailment is "roomatism"—one resident accuses the other of stealing articles that have been misplaced; one opens the windows and the other closes it. Although we know that there are psychological reasons for these accusations, nevertheless much bickering could be avoided. It would be advisable, too, to allow the resident to bring along with him some favorite item of furniture or accessories which would add to the feeling that this is his own home, and some consideration of his personality should be shown in the furnishing of the room. In addition to the well-equipped kitchens for general use, small kitchenettes on the floors can be provided so that a resident can make himself a cup of tea or coffee. Dining rooms for ambulatory patients must be thoughtfully planned so that they do not resemble army "mess halls." A dining room that seats one hundred or more people may impress a visitor, but is uncomfortable for the aged. Small rooms, attractively decorated, with tables for two or four, make for congenial conversation and a pleasant interlude at mealtime.

Entrance halls and corridors should be built so that residents in wheelchairs can be wheeled in and out of doors. The grounds should be leveled so as to enable and encourage people to spend more time outdoors, and to take walks when weather permits. In the well-planned home there would be areas for gardening in the proper season, and pleasant, well-landscaped areas just for sitting out.

A number of older people find great comfort and solace in religious services, and a chapel in an institution for the aged serves their needs. Although residents should not be pressured to attend services, they can be gently encouraged to do so and particularly to pray for others. This can help many of them to avoid concentrating upon themselves, as so many do, to the point of becoming hypochondriacs. The chapel should also offer solace to relatives of the residents in time of stress, as when their beloved ones are about to embark upon the inevitable journey of all mankind.

Since safety of the residents is of uppermost concern, every measure must be taken to safeguard their health and to prevent accidents. This involves such items as fire protection, with complete sprinkler installation. Bathrooms are the source of many accidents, but there are many devices which may be employed as preventive and protective measures: there need not be locks on doors, tubs should have safety rails to assist residents getting in and out of them, fragile enamel and porcelain handles must be avoided, and hot water must be thermostat-controlled so that the old people will not suffer burns. Special attention should be given to floors, with nonskid materials used to avoid accidents. The corridors must be provided with night lights for frequent trips to the bathrooms, and with handrails for assistance in walking. In the bedrooms, too, safeguards are mandatory; for example, placing beds against walls, with bedrails on outside edges.

Provisions for Medical Care of Residents

The foregoing suggestions for comfort and safety lead us to the primary concern in the program of an institution for the aged—the medical care to be provided for residents. As people get older, their health needs increase. They require personal health services widely varying in type, scope, amount, and duration. They need twice as much hospital care as younger people, and if these needs are to be met, the institution must have adequate facilities, techniques, equipment, and professional and auxiliary personnel. It is desirable, whenever possible, for the institution to be affiliated with a well-eqipped hospital, and if it is a teaching hospital with medical-school affiliations, this is of mutual benefit to all concerned. The physician-in-chief of the institution may be appointed with the advice of the medical executive committee of the hospital, and a joint program for the health of the residents can be worked out in association with the hospital staff. An example of this type of planning, with which I have had personal and gratifying experience, was a program in which consultants in the various branches of medicine were invited to hold clinics in the institution. This brought an out-patient type of service into the home, instead of carrying patients back and forth to the hospitals. An affiliation with a well-staffed and well-equipped hospital also brings a feeling of satisfaction in knowing that there is an ever-ready bed for any situation in which a patient has to be hospitalized. The hospital, too, benefits from such an association in that it offers an opportunity for ever-expanding research in the new and fruitful field of gerontology.

The medical staff of the institution should include, in addition to an adequate daytime staff, a resident physician on duty at night in order to provide twenty-four-hour coverage.

The infirmary of a home for the aged should be fully equipped in every area to provide for minor surgery, various injuries, and all types of ambulatory ailments. In addition to physician's offices, and those of medical secretaries, there must be provisions for the storing of medical records, which should always be complete. There should be an x-ray room with well-installed modern equipment, and a clinical laboratory for routine urinalyses and blood chemical determinations as well as for electrocardiography—in charge of full-time medical technicians. A pharmacy room, properly supervised, must contain the sickroom supplies, pharmaceuticals, drugs and vaccines, to be available at all times. The infirmary can have wards of four beds to a room for the acutely ill, some isolation rooms for contagious disease, and a room for terminal cases.

A modern physiotherapy department under the supervision of a full-time therapist adds immeasurably to the therapeutic regimen and also provides physical comfort and mental encouragement.

A modern, well-equipped, brightly furnished dental room should be provided for the treatment and extraction of teeth, and for the fitting of dentures.

A podiatrist is essential in any medical program for the care of the aged because the feet of older persons require a great deal of attention. The aged are more insensitive to heat and to cold, wound healing is retarded due to poor circulation, there is loss of fat padding on the soles, and the skin of the toes becomes thinner. Aged people also have chronic progressive degenerative diseases that predispose their feet to gangrene. Proper foot care is essential to patients with diabetes and vascular disease. These services, which may seem of minor value to many of us, are of great importance to the aged because of enhanced comfort and an increased sense of well-being.

A program for the complete care of the aged must include a well-equipped department of occupational therapy, with trained personnel. Residents come to this area to renew former activities and to learn new skills. To work is living, but to be idle is boredom. Every resident, even the nonambulatory, can be encouraged to participate in some form of occupational therapy.

The medical staff should include a psychiatrist—an essential service for the welfare of the aged. Not all mental illnesses in the aged are due to "organic brain syndrome," as so many mental manifestations are incorrectly labeled. A number of these patients suffer from functional illness and are amenable to electric shock therapy with little more hazard than in younger patients. Some of the mental symptoms are manifestations of physical disorders, such as anemia, uremia, dehydration, diabetes, or the toxemia of infection. When the underlying conditions are improved, many mental symptoms disappear. To differentiate between organic and functional mental syndromes is often difficult, but the cooperative effort of physician and psychiatrist can solve many of these problems. The newly developed tranquilizers, used with caution, are often of great value in these situations.

Phases of the Medical Program

The four phases of a medical program in an institution for the aged are: (1) preventive, (2) curative, (3) rehabilitative, and (4) environmental.

Preventive phase. This involves a periodic examination of each resident every six months, in order to detect early signs and symptoms of preventable disease. For example, control of obesity can be attempted before damage is done, and treatment of diabetes or anemias can be started in the early stages of these diseases. All types of immunizations, such as those for influenza, can be given. Cataracts detected early can be removed before total blindness develops, and hearing losses can be helped by hearing aids or operations.

Curative phase. The medical care of the aged should be continuous rather than symptomatic and occasional. It is not a matter of merely keeping a patient quiet or subdued and the prescribing of a cathartic. Older people are entitled to the advances of modern medicine with all their attendant benefits. A single standard of medical care is indicated for all age groups. Old age is no contraindication to surgical procedures, and neither is coronary disease. One must consider the cardiac status, and the decision should be reached by a total evaluation of each individual case. Usually the aged do not fear death, but they do dread an operation—probably because of the fear of "self-mutilation," according to the psychologists. Symptomatology in the aged is often somewhat different from that in other age groups, i.e., the full clinical picture may not be evident. This situation is found in the development of a myocardial infarct, or in a case of appendicitis which may progress to perforation without the vaguest hint of abdominal pain, with little or no fever, and with a normal leukocyte count.

Drug therapy for a geriatric patient, in a sense, corresponds to that for a pediatric patient. Both exhibit striking drug suscepti-bility. In the older patient with peptic ulcer, large doses of atropine may cause glaucoma; and in the older patient with an enlarged prostate plus urinary obstruction and residual urine, bromides may be reabsorbed and ultimately cause a toxic state. Caution must be exercised in prescribing sleeping medication, because the aged, especially those who are sedentary, chronically complain of insomnia. Factors to be carefully considered are the size, the dosage, the interval between administrations, and the side effects of every drug.

Rehabilitative phase. The rehabilitation of the patient is of great importance in modern medicine. At the termination of the acute stage of the disease, it is the doctor's task to alleviate and eliminate any mental and physical sequelae due to disuse. Active and passive exercises must be started and continued. If neces-sary, new functions may be developed if the old ones are lost. This is best illustrated in cases of cerebrovascular accidents. As soon as the acute stage of the illness is over, the patient (out of bed) is started on a series of treatments and new learning processes. If he is left with paralysis of one arm, he can be trained to use the other. The occupational therapy department can be well utilized in this connection, along with the services of the physiotherapists.

Environmental phase. The environment of the aged patient is of extreme importance in assisting him to retain his individuality. Regimentation of any sort must be avoided, and he should be free to come and go as he wishes, in accordance with his physical and mental status. He should be represented in decisions made concerning him and his care. Attempts to raise the usually low morale of the ill resident must be made by all in attendance. Personnel selected to care for the elderly need to show sympathy and understanding so that the patients will be encouraged.

Physical Activity

Physical activity is a necessity for the aged because inactivity affects the mind as well as the body. Physical inactivity is reflected in altered kidney function, cardiac output, lessened activity of the gastrointestinal tract, and in weakness and diminished tone of the body musculature. Mental activity must constantly be encouraged, and can be aided by occupational and recreational therapy. There must be an effort to stimulate and develop more reading, study, and group activity. There is no more miserable sight than a group of elderly people sitting in a dayroom unattended, unoccupied, and often dressed in nightgowns. A person's dignity is restored by his being dressed in his best clothes and his walking shoes. All of these details help to create a psychological climate involving respect for his personality, and this is a powerful factor in rebuilding the mind. Activity during the day promotes sleep at night; thus the need for sedatives will be reduced. Idleness leads to apathy and eventually to depression. A person must be involved in a program commensurate with his capacity and his ability.

Nutrition

One of the real enjoyments of the aged is the consumption of food, and consequently most of them eat too much at a time when their caloric requirement is diminishing. The important element is the quality and the composition of the diet, as worked out by the dietitian. The diet should contain all the foods the old person needs for bulk and elimination, but in proper relation to his decreased carbohydrate tolerance and his difficulties in absorbing fat. In this way, although calories consumed will be lessened and the obese will lose some weight, individual weights on the whole will be preserved. This is very important, since excessive loss of weight in the older person requires searching for other than a dietary cause.

The dietitian should direct the preparation and presentation of food in an attractive and appetizing manner. This will not only increase the joy of eating, but will afford the aged the consideration they need to maintain dignity. The dietitian will also supervise the diets of the diabetics, and of those who require salt-free or low-fat meals.

Social Work and Recreation

There are other essential services in an institution for the aged. A most valuable addition to the staff of a home for the aged is the social worker. From the time of a resident's application for admission, the social worker's services are involved. Physicians and social workers jointly will decide whether the application is to be processed, and if so, whether it should be given priority. On entering the home, the resident must be given immediate casework service to aid in his adjustment to his new environment. There should be an orientation process of about six weeks, and every effort made to establish all the facts of his physical and mental condition. Social adjustment and requirements for such service will be decided at that time. Most people who enter an institution feel lost in their new environment, e.g., some of them cannot adjust to the change from living alone to living within a group, and others harbor bitter feelings toward relatives who, they feel, have abandoned them. The social worker can be of great value at this time, both to the incoming resident and to his relatives, who may feel some guilt about placing a parent in the home. The incoming residents are often annoyed by the older residents, and are quick to complain and become hostile and depressed. The social worker's services are of inestimable help in this transition period. A number of residents require continuing counseling service from time to time as emotional problems develop, e.g., anxiety about deterioration of their physical condition or an increased frequency of intermittent disease.

Other helpful services in an institution will include a barber shop for men and a beauty parlor for women, to enable them to be better groomed and to add to their sense of well-being. For their mental health, it is advisable to set aside a room as a library, well stocked with books suited to the individual taste; here, a person can get away for a while and find solace in reading. Much pleasure can also be derived from having a soundproof room where records can be played without disturbing others. This stimulates the minds of the aged residents by recalling pleasant experiences of the past, and also gives a spiritual lift which is of therapeutic value.

Summary

An ever-increasing number of people are living past the biblical age of threescore and ten. Many are not able to remain in the ideal place for an aged person—his own home and his own environment. Therefore it is necessary to provide an institutional atmosphere which will approximate that of the former environment as far as possible. No aged person should be put into an institution from choice, but rather from necessity. Our entire attitude toward the aged must be reorientated to accept the fact that debility and disease are not synonymous with old age. Old age is not a disease, and a diagnosis of "old age" should not be made. There should be a single standard of medical and health care for all age groups.

A person admitted to a home for the aged must be provided with all possible safety measures, and with medical care by an adequate, properly trained medical staff who work as a team, with understanding and sympathy. The personality and individuality of the aged resident must be respected, and this should be reflected in his care and environment. The four phases of the medical program—preventive, curative, rehabilitative, and environmental—plus auxiliary services, combine to add life and pleasure to old person's added years and to make those years more meaningful.

PART III

Case Histories, Diagnostic, Techniques, and Other Medical Matters

Medical History as a Prophylactic

In 1908 Dr. William Osler revisted Vienna. He sent back a letter intended for the American medical profession. In typical Oslerian manner he wrote of an interview granted with Minerva Medica. He boldly suggested that she cross the Atlantic and set up her temple in the New World. The patroness of the physician and the goddess of health replied, "We gods have but one motto—those that honor us, we honor. Give me the temples, give me the priests, give me the true worship, the old Hippocratic service of the art and science of ministering to man, and I will come. By the eternal law under which we gods live, I would have to come."

In this charming, whimsical manner, Dr. Osler uttered a prophecy which is being fulfilled before our own eyes. Minerva has crossed the Atlantic and is one of the numerous refugees in the United States. The pillars of most temples of learning in Europe are tottering and a great many seats of culture are laid waste. Many of the priests of those temples are scattered over the world. Some have found a haven in this country. Those left behind are muzzled and their creative powers dampened. The United States is becoming the center of research in all fields of learning.

The temples of scientific research are here in large numbers and the quality and quantity of work superior to that being done

First published in *Diplomate*, November 1943.

anywhere in the world. This is true of all the arts and sciences, and medicine, with its numerous ramifications, is no exception to the general trend. The bibiographies of our current medical scientific papers, unlike in the years past, are mainly American references, sprinkled here and there with a few European authors.

But medicine is unlike any other science. Whereas the personality and traits of the scientist are of little concern in other fields of endeavor, in medicine the physician himself plays an important part. Medicine has always been, and always will remain, an art as well as a science. In ministering to the sick, the art is equally as important as the science. All the accumulated scientific data in a particular ailment are only tools in the hands of the doctor in charge of the case. The physician has a great duty and responsibility, and in numerous instances is the final judge as well as prosecutor. "How" he does is often as important as "what" he does. A distinguished dean of one of our leading medical schools once welcomed the incoming freshman class with the following words, "Gentlemen, you are entering upon the study of a profession in which you are responsible to God and to your conscience." Our daily medical experiences reveal the truth of the above remarks.

Now to attain priesthood in the temple of Minerva, the physician must not only be equipped with the facts of the fundamental medical sciences, but he must also have a personality of high quality and high purpose. Medical history, it seems to me, can serve in some ways to develop these high qualities in the physician, as well as to prevent to some extent certain personality defects. These can be best attained by inculcating in medical students an interest in medical history.

First of all, medical history provides a cultural background for the physician. The study of history leads to a certain maturity of intellectual development. One who does not know what has gone on in the past is, to some extent, still a child mentally. Certainly the physician to whom patients come to reveal body and soul ought to be of sufficient maturity to cope with those problems.

The numerous facts in medicine studied from a historical evolutionary process begin to synthesize and group themselves into definite shapes and forms. Isolated facts are like scattered leaves, but when viewed from a historical point of view, they group themselves into foliage, trunk, branches, and roots, which form one kind of a tree. Isolated medical eponyms are just so many disjointed facts to be committed to memory. But once the life of the physician and his original contribution are studied, these same facts stand out as a living picture in one's memory. Percussion, auscultation, Skoda's resonance, and Traube's semilunar space are just additions to an already burdensome nomenclature. But the stories of Auerbruger, Laënnec, Skoda, and Traube are fascinating tales never to be forgotten.

This experiment in medical history has been tried for several years with some sections of students in physical diagnosis. Each student has been required to investigate one historical fact, read an original paper, and submit a summary to the group. The actual reading of the reports takes only about ten minutes. These students have felt that they were well rewarded for the extra time spent. The same method could be applied in all other medical courses. Wherever possible, the historical background of a certain subject should be emphasized and the original contributions used as an assignment to the students. Lectures on medical history should be provided so that the students' curiosity for historical data may be aroused. If all these attempts fail to arouse an interest in the student, then the fault lies with the student himself. The late Harvey Cushing demonstrated this fact. It is told that a student came to him for examination in order to obtain a surgical internship. Instead of questioning him on certain surgical procedures, Cushing asked him to name the originators of the methods of percussion and auscultation. He felt, no doubt, that one who had the intellectual curiosity to delve into these medical origins had most certainly learned the facts obviously essential to the pursuit of his profession.

It is obvious that medical history does broaden the base of the medical sciences. Furthermore, as in the construction of any edifice, the greater the planned height above the ground, the deeper must be the foundation. This is true of all branches of learning, but even more so in medicine. But medical history can serve a greater and nobler purpose in the character building of the physician himself. It will, to a certain degree, prevent him from acquiring certain deleterious and undignified traits. It will, in a sense, act as a prophylactic in character development.

After all, physicians are mortal and subject to all of the frailties of human beings. But the physician needs greater strength of character to resist the many temptations to which a weakling may easily succumb. There are ever present the tempting desire to accumulate wealth and the enticing craving for fame. These energies can be guided to bring benefits to all mankind, or they may blind one's vision and lead one astray. But there is another deleterious effect which, if not checked, comes from the inner self of the physician. The doctor, by the mere nature of his profession, has a certain degree of power over his fellow men, who come to him in times of all kinds of trouble. Patients place themselves in his hands, and not only expose their physical bodies for examination, but reveal their innermost souls. This not only grants him power, but may lead to a feeling of superiority over his fellow men, and if not checked this may develop into undignified pomposity and vanity. This in itself would be harmless even though unbecoming. But an inflated ego, like a malignant growth which invades other tissues, over-steps all who come in contact with it. Patients as well as colleagues suffer from a physician who allows his pomposity to go unbridled. Like a growth once detected, this should be eradicated. Is it not evident at times in the young medical student when he first puts on his white coat and is allowed to take a history and examine a patient? And on hearing himself called "doctor" by the patient, he begins to feel his superiority. If perchance, heaven forbid, he makes a correct diagnosis (usually with the aid of the various technical tests which a hospital is equipped to do), which is different from the diagnosis made by the physician on the case, he feels so much the better man than the L.M.D. If not checked, this is carried on throughout his career. A senior staff member told that he met an intern in the corridor of a hospital. He greeted his young colleague in a friendly manner, and the young man told him that on getting through with his internship, he intended to open an office for the practice of medicine. The young intern then asked the doctor how often he would call him in consultation.

To be ambitious to attain fame is a noble quality if pursued in a humble and honorable manner. When one studies the lives of really great men, it is obvious that they were natural and meek. Dr. Carl Ludwig Schleich, who worked in the laboratory of the great Paul Ehrlich, wrote of this mastermind in medicine as follows: "For any student of character, he was a living proof of the fact that true greatness has no need of pose or concealment or of pretense." Modesty and humility are the very attributes of a scholar. When the Book of Books summarized the greatness of the first doctor of public health, Moses, it merely said, "And the man Moses was very humble." The reverse seems also to be true. No sooner does a person begin to pose and show superiority at every step, then one realizes that he has little more to offer. He has reached his maximum of achievement.

Now medical history makes the physician conscious of the fact that he is entering a profession which has a tradition of three thousand years. We know what an inspiring force it is to be conscious of belonging to that great international family of physicians. This is where the sense of *noblesse oblige* should be aroused. Medical history brings him into communion with the great spirits of medical men of all times. It makes the great masters one's contemporaries. In numerous instances, the very lives of these men throughout the long journey of medicine are models to be emulated. In the light of medical history, one's ego is deflated. One's shadow is smallest when the sun is directly overhead, and so does one feel humble in the presence of a galaxy of the great personalities of the past. We learn that real fame is not acquired by knowing the right person on some newspaper staff and having one's name appear in the daily press. Nor is immortality attained in every instance by publishing a paper, or papers, or even books. Overemphasis is, at the present time, placed on the number of articles one publishes, while other criteria are overlooked. This is another goal to strive for in medicine—if pursued honorably and conscientiously—even though but one small fact is added to our store of knowledge. Because this is how each generation brings its contribution to the benefits of mankind. To attain such a position, the real contributor must divorce himself from the idea of self-glorification. The latter aim may lead to ignoble acts in order to gain publicity.

A glance at the physicians in medical history will reveal that the great souls, in their search for truth, had no regard for themselves. Many have risked everything and have dared to tell the truth. It took a great deal of courage on the part of Oliver Wendell Holmes to proclaim that a physician carried the disease of puerperal fever from one patient to another. A study of medical history will help to bring home the fact that not everything that is written or published is a classic, and that a physician must not be measured by paper weight. An overabundance of foliage often conceals a lack of fruit.

In the study of medical history, one becomes acquainted with a long list of intellectual giants who come to life again. One who studies their lives and their works becomes conscious of ever being in their company. One weighs his words in the presence of the real great. Furthermore, medical history holds the keys to the portals of the Hall of Fame, where physicians enter by invitation and not by self-proclamation. Even the shouting of the mob does not help to crash the gates.

A study of medical history will reveal that the so-called medical code of ethics is not merely a number of rules to handicap either the physician or the public, but is a natural outgrowth of the very nature of the profession. On the contrary, the standards of medical tradition allow for the growth and development of the physician and at the same time safeguard the public. Medicine, by its very mission, does demand of every physician to at least aim at being a saint. Yet the physician must be very humble as he goes about his tasks. As Prof. Frances Greenwood Peabody wrote about President Charles W. Elliot, "The saints, he felt, would never become saintly until they forgot their saintliness."

Now, snobbishness in any other profession may produce a comic caricature to be laughed at. Being a snob and marrying the boss's daughter may lead to success in some other calling, but in medicine it may injure some sensitive patients as well as stunt medical progress. A promising scholar of noble character may be crushed in an interview for admission to a medical school if the one in charge is not of the highest type.

Again, the young physician looks to his seniors not only for guidance, but also for inspiration. A new thought is like a young, budding plant. Whether it will burst into flower depends upon how it is handled. A bud picked by the gentle hand of a wise gardener, placed in a kindly and well-watered soil, thrives and flourishes and sprouts forth into bloom. The same bud stepped upon by a crude foot dies. A newly inspired idea can be killed by unsympathetic words. The doctor who is truly great can bring out the best in the younger generation. Viscount Grey, in a lecture delivered at Harvard some years ago, tells the following episode: "Not long ago, when an English friend of mine was dying, his business agent came over to see him. One of the family asked the agent whether he had come on important business. 'No,' he said, 'I have come for a little conversation because I was feeling depressed this morning and I wanted to be made to feel two inches taller.' "

This thought can be utilized as a measuring rod to gauge the real greatness of a physician. In the presence of great and modest men, the young who come for advice grow in stature, while in the presence of others one is humiliated and shrinks. The patient, too, senses this encouraging or depressing air of the physician. Patients are exhilarated in the presence of some physicians and are mentally crushed by others, no matter how technically skilled they are. The physician who has attained prominence in a certain field of medicine in consultation on a serious problem will show his greatness by his humility and kindness. He comes as a friend and guide to the patient and the physician in the case alike, and not merely to impress any one of his superiority. One of the learned doctors of the Talmud expressed it in a beautiful manner which can serve as a guide even at the present time. He said, "Do not resemble a big door, which lets in the wind, or a small door, which makes the worthy bend down; but resemble the threshold on which all may tread, or a low peg on which all can hang their things."

This humility can best be shown when a young physician with a problem to be solved looks to his older colleagues for guidance. The following is a fine example of how nobly it can be done.

A world-famous scholar, whose knowledge is not only profound but vast, and includes the mastery of several ancient languages and their literatures, shows a fine sense of humility in his relationship toward his students. Borrowing a phrase from Dr. Oliver Wendell Holmes, who spoke of his professorship as not being a chair but a settee, this professor could occupy an endowed bench. To this scholar the entire field of learning in the so-called Dark Ages is a source of illumination on all of our modern problems in the arts and sciences. Yet when a graduate or an undergraduate student comes in for guidance or advice, he meets him as an equal and is free with counsel and suggestion. A colleague once asked this teacher, "Why do you give away so many good suggestions?" This scholar replied, "There are plenty of ideas—enough for all of us." Such are the generosity and encouragement of a true scholar—revealed by his modesty and humility. Such is the type of teacher and physician we need for our temples of medicine, if we want Minerva to stay here.

A similar example was to be found in the late Prof. Francis W. Peabody, of the Harvard Medical School. This inspiring teacher, busy as he was with teaching, research, and executive work, found time to encourage the young. A medical student gave him a reprint of a paper on medical history. He was not too busy to sit down and read the article, and then write the student the following: "Thank you very much for the reprint of your article. . . . I have read it with much interest and I think it shows very clearly what I have never entirely understood . . ." Such are the words of a person that was great, yet humble.*

An outstanding example of this encouragement to the young was the case of the young orthopedic surgeon Banting, who went to Prof. J. J. MacLeod with an idea. This resulted in giving insulin to the world, and to the great good fortune of humanity. What would have happened had he gone to someone unsympathetic and uninterested?

I wish to conclude with the words of a practicing physician and great philosopher of the Middle Ages, namely, Naḥmanides, also known as Bonastrug da Porta (1194–1270). In this ethical letter addressed to his son, he praises humility:

Hear, my son, the instruction of thy father, and forsake not the law of thy mother. My son, my beloved, accustom thyself always to speak gently to every man, at all times and seasons; thereby thou shalt avoid anger, which is a very bad and blameworthy disposition, for it leads to

*See above, p. 85, for a biographical study of Francis W. Peabody.

sin, as our teachers of blessed memory said: "If one gets angry, it is regarded as if he worshipped idols." And all punishments of Gehenna have power over him, as it is written: "Remove anger from thy heart, and put away evil from thy flesh." By the word evil, Gehenna is meant, as it is written: "Even the wicked for the day of evil." When thou avoidest anger, thou wilt bring to thy mind the quality of humility, and cleave upon it, for it is the best of all virtues, as it is written: "The reward of humility is the fear of the Lord." The Mishnah likewise says: "Be exceedingly humble of spirit." Even our teacher Moses, peace be upon him, was praised by this quality, as it is written: "And the man Moses was very meek." It is also through the merit of this virtue that the Torah was given at his hand, and that he was called the teacher of all prophets. He who attains unto this quality is beloved of Heaven, as it is written: "With him also that is of a contrite and humble spirit." When thou clingest to the quality of humility, the fear of God will come to thy mind; for thou wilt continually lay to thy heart whence thou camest, and whither thou art going (thou art worm and maggot in thy life and in thy death), and before whom thou art destined to render account and reckoning (before the supreme King of Kings, the Holy One, blessed be He, whose glory fills the earth). It is also written: "Do not I fill heaven and earth? said the Lord." It is also written: "Behold, heaven and the heaven of heavens cannot contain Thee; how much less the hearts of the children of men!" When thou wilt consider all this, thou wilt fear thy Creator, and guard thyself against sin. By clinging to these qualities, thou wilt be in a state of perfection and sublimity, and wilt continually be happy with thy lot; this latter, too, is one of the good qualities, as the Mishnah says: "Who is rich? he who rejoices in his lot." If thy conduct is according to the quality of humility and thou art ashamed before every man, and thou fearest thy Creator, who gives thee life, so that thou sinnest not, the spirit of the Shekhinah and the splendor of its glory will dwell upon thee, and thou wilt deserve the life of this world and of the world to come.

My son and my beloved, know assuredly that one who exalts himself above his fellow men rebels against the kingdom of heaven, for he makes use of God's garment, as it is written: "The Lord reigneth, He is clothed with pride." And God, who is blessed, says concerning the haughty man: "I and he cannot dwell together in this world." Accordingly he who is haughty will be uprooted from the world.

He requests his son to read this epistle with his friend once a week. It would do us well if all of us dedicated to the service should periodically examine ourselves in the light of medical history. It would not only broaden our knowledge, but would instill in us the sense of humility which is so essential to scholarship and the progress of learning. It would make us worthy of the high worship of Minerva, and assure her permanent stay in this country.

The Cultural Background of the Patient as Part of the Physician's Armamentarium

Four Case Studies

In the works of Plato, in the *Charmides,* we find the following amazing passage:

"But our king Zamolxis," said he, "being a god, says that, as it is not proper to attempt to cure the eyes without the head, nor the head without the body, so neither is it proper to cure the body without the soul; and that this was the reason why many diseases escape the Greek physicians, because they are ignorant of the whole, to which attention ought to be paid; for when this is not in a good state, it is impossible for a part to be well."

Yet it is only recently that the medical profession has finally accepted the interrelationship of mind and body and has developed the so-called psychosomatic medicine. It seems to me that many ailments still escape us at the present time as they did in the time of the Greek physicians, for our knowledge of

First published in *Journal of Abnormal and Social Psychology,* April 1952.

somatic disturbances is far more advanced than our understanding of the psyche of the patient.

The modern doctor's bag contains a number of drugs and ampules to meet practically every drastic emergency. His armamentarium also contains some tools of investigation to aid in diagnostic purposes. Tissues and fluids are subjected to the finest chemical analysis possible. For it is only in such a manner that we begin to unravel the secrets of nature that are concealed in the living organism. Now if the cultural background of his patient is also stored in the physician's mind, it will often help him to understand and analyze his patient's troubles, and thus to arrive at a right diagnosis. At times he may utilize this cultural background as a rapid, rational therapeutic measure. There are cases, as we shall show, where the rational processes of the patient are blocked either by fear or some other emotional complex. Here is a method by which an approach is made to the reasoning processes of the patient by way of a detour—through the open door of the underground cultural storehouse. The ideal physician, then, will not only sympathize with his patient, but as in art, he will possess empathy for him. Whereas sympathy is a feeling with a subject—what the Germans call *mitfühlen*; he will also have empathy or feeling into *einfühlen*. By understanding thoroughly the cultural background of a patient, the physician feels into the very depths of the mind of a patient. He understands his intricate complexities and so can help the patient to untangle himself from the web of troublesome perplexities that the patient spins around himself.

The following are a group of four cases from my private practice which illustrate the value of understanding the cultural background of a patient.

Case I

Mrs. R.C., age sixty, housewife, came to see me on April 9, 1947. Her chief complaint was nervousness of one year's duration. Her present illness had begun about one year before when she would awaken suddenly from her sleep and find her body muscles stiff, particularly in the back of the neck. There were no recent loss of weight and no other symptoms. She denied having any mental worries.

P.H. Was born in Russia. Since the age of seven she has been residing in the United States. Thirty-five years ago she had pulmonary tuberculosis for which she was confined to a sanatorium for ten months. No previous operations. Six years ago she fell and sprained her right hip.

M.H. Married thirty-five years. Has one son living and well. Her husband is also living and well.

F.H. Father died of heart trouble at the age of forty-five. Mother died of pulmonary tuberculosis at the age of thirty-one. One sister is living and well.

Head. Claims that she feels dizzy, no headaches.

C.R. Has no cough. No precordial pain. Claims that she sweats somewhat at night.

G.I. Appetite good. Bowels are regular with the aid of laxatives. No G.U. symptoms. Says weight was over 200 pounds thirty years ago.

Physical examination. Revealed a well-developed, well-nourished woman; weight—164 pounds; throat—clear; eyes—negative; eye-grounds—negative; ears—negative; heart was not enlarged, rate—72, rhythm—regular, no murmurs; BP 160/ 180; lungs—slight dullness over right apex; no rales; abdomen—negative; reflexes—normal. In other words, the physical examination was essentially negative.

In spite of the fact that she denied having any worries, a detailed history of her life revealed the following story: Thirty-five years ago she had pulmonary tuberculosis for which she was confined to a sanatorium. On leaving the sanatorium she was told not to have children as it might reactivate her tuberculous lesion. In spite of this medical advice she took a chance and became pregnant and gave birth to a son. She gave her son the best education possible in spite of financial stress. He graduated from law school and passed the bar. During World War II he volunteered and served in the United States Army. Upon his discharge from the army he was married and made his home in the West.

Upon questioning as to whether she sees him, she replied, "He lives too far." In telling about her son the patient spoke reluctantly and without feeling. On further pressing of the question of how often she visits him, she finally said, "They don't want to see me!—I lost him." When asked to explain, she said that he had married out of his faith and was lost. The patient then became silent. Here I felt that the first indications of the cause of her symptoms were brought to the surface. Here was a mother who had risked her life in order to have a child. She gave all to him—in care and education. Finally, in intermarrying—in view of her Orthodox beliefs—she considered him lost.

An attempt was now made to integrate that problem in her emotional thinking and make her feel that she still possessed him. At first an attempt was made to appeal to her maternal instinct. I asked her if she would feel better if she had received a communication from the War Department telling her that her son was missing in action. At first there was no response, but on further questioning she remarked, "If you insist, I don't know." In other words, this episode, to her, was equivalent to death; and what was worse, death with disgrace instead of glory. A final appeal was made by telling her the following story. The patient was told to listen carefully to every word for she would be questioned about it afterwards (The story "One Must Ask for Mercy," is from the Hebrew by a Palestinian author, the late Moshe Ben Eliezer.)

There was a small town in Russia which was famous for its rabbi. He was a scholar and an authority in the law as well as a saint in the mode of living. Many large cities were competing to obtain him as their spiritual leader, but to no avail. His oldest daughter, who was married to a merchant, lived in the capital of czarist Russia, St. Petersburg. Her two children, a son and a daughter, attended the Imperial University. While there, they were involved in a revolutionary plot, a plot that was planned against the life of the Czar himself. They were caught and it was well known in those days that the sentence would be death. The parents spent money and effort but to no avail. All doors were closed to them. When all attempts had failed, the daughter came rushing home to seek aid from her father. On seeing her the old man sensed that his daughter was in trouble and said to himself, "When all is well with children you neither see them nor seldom hear from them; but when they are in trouble they hurry home." [Here my patient became very attentive and completely absorbed in the story.] With tears in her eyes the daughter told him of her plight.

"But what can I, a rabbi, do in such a case? the father asked.

Then the daughter proceeded to tell him that in the capital there was a man who was very influential among the dignitaries of the royal court, and that only he could save their lives.

"This man is very stern and unapproachable, but perhaps you—an old rabbi—can prevail upon him for help."

The poor, old rabbi made the long journey to St. Petersburg and finally located and gained an interview with this influential person. The rabbi told him his tale of woe—of his two grandchildren who were facing death.

"What was the crime?" asked the man.

"Revolution," answered the rabbi.

"For every crime one can find an excuse," shouted the man, "but revolution, why that undermines the very foundation of government!"

The rabbi lowered his head in sorrow, not knowing what to say.

The man continued, "The Czar, his excellency, can find no excuse for a rebel nor does the fact that one comes from a great family help the matter. Very often members of the royal family were condemned and executed."

The rabbi listened, his face white as snow, and his eyes seemed to express the agony of hopelessness.

Here the man tapped him on the shoulder and said, "Even so, one must ask for mercy. Meet me tomorrow at the royal court and I shall attempt to appeal the case for you."

The man fulfilled his promise. He made a plea, and as a result the children were set free.

Having fulfilled his mission, the rabbi was about to return to his home; but, he felt that he must first go to the man and express his gratitude for saving two lives. He entered the man's home, and when the man saw him, he greeted the rabbi cordially and asked him to follow him. The rabbi followed him from one room to another; finally he took out a key, opened a door, and again said, "Follow me." He locked the door behind them. This was his private library. To the amazement of the rabbi, he found the shelves filled with tomes of ancient Hebrew literature—the Sacred Writings, the Mishnah, the Talmud.

"Rabbi," said the man, "This is my private sanctum sanctorum. No stranger has ever crossed this threshold. It is here that I find relaxation from my daily routine. Rabbi, I was born a Jew; but I am converted and very few know about it. Do you think, Rabbi, that there is any chance for me?"

The rabbi looked at him and said, "For every sin one may repent on the Day of Atonement and the sin may be absolved; but conversion, why that destroys the very foundation of religion!"

The man turned pale.

Then the rabbi tapped him on his shoulder and said, "Even so, one must ask for mercy . . ."

At the end of the story, the woman burst into tears and laughter at the same time. She got up and said, "I am very happy that I came to see you." Nothing was said after that.

She was given a simple tonic. Two weeks later she called me on the telephone and said, "I have been sleeping nights and feel much better. Do you think I should refill that medicine?" She was told that she no longer needed it.

The patient visited me again on July 11, 1947. At that time she was well adjusted to her problem. On questioning her about her son, she said that he was very happily married and living a life of his own.

"My husband is visiting him now, and when he returns I shall visit him myself."

This case was discussed with a prominent Boston psychiatrist. On completion of my story he asked in amazement, "How did you find a story that could fit the case so perfectly?"

"I didn't," I replied, "I found a patient whose case fitted a story which I had read."

Case II

Mr. F.P.N., age fifty-one, came to my office on November 3, 1936. His chief complaint was pain in the chest, coming on with exertion and relieved by rest. Pain radiated to the left arm.

P.H. Irrelevant except for pneumonia at the age of thirty.

F.H. Father died at the age of fifty-one of pneumonia. Mother died at the age of forty-seven of cancer.

M.H. Married, has three children living and well.

Physical examination. Revealed an obese, keen, emotionally tense, businessman of about fifty-one years of age; weight—193 pounds; vital capacity 3,000 cc; hemoglobin 95%; blood pressure 200/102.

Diagnosis of hypertension, hypertensive heart disease, and angina pectoris was made.

The patient was advised to go to bed for three weeks. He was also advised to lose some weight.

At the end of three weeks he was allowed to get up but was advised to retire from his business. He continued to have some precordial pain even on rest, for he was tense and aggravated. Whatever one told him to do his reply was, "What difference does it make? In six months I shall be in Wakefield." (There was a family plot in the cemetery in Wakefield.) He seemed resigned to death. It was felt that if we could overcome his resignation and instill some hopefulness in him, it would help his condition.

Instead of discussing his condition with him, I told him about the romance of the rebuilding of Palestine—how a new life was starting there; how Hebrew was being rejuvenated; and how Jews were continuing to create a literature which is a continuation of the Bible. As he became absorbed in the pioneering drama, I interrupted the story by saying to him, "Do you know what I would like you to do? It would also please your wife very much, for you know her deep religious emotions. I would like to take a trip with you in five years from today, to Palestine, thus giving him a goal.

This suggestion took root and it worked well. I called it a "five-year plan for angina pectoris."

At the end of six months, on one of my routine visits, he said, "Four and one-half years more, Doctor."

A year later he said, "Three and one-half years more to go." And so he looked forward to that goal. In December 1941 I said, smilingly, "What about the trip?"

And he replied, "How can we go now, with hell breaking loose all over the world?"

So we agreed to let the plan go for another five years—until the world again would return to normal.

Meanwhile, another tragedy occurred. In 1942 his youngest son, who resided in the West, accidentally shot himself while cleaning his rifle. His married daughter received the sad news by telephone at 4:00 A.M. She in turn called me at that hour to go and break the news to her father, who was suffering from as severe an ailment as angina pectoris. As a physician, I felt it was my duty—one which I could not shirk. At that time the patient was retired and lived in an apartment hotel. I knew that his usual habit was to rise early in the morning and sit in the lobby. I told the daughter to meet me there, and we would go together to break the sad news. I entered the lobby followed by the daughter, and as he saw me enter he said, "What happened?"

To which I said, "I have some sad news to tell you, but first I want to ask you for a favor. Cooperate with me so as to save your wife, you know that she is emotionally very tense."

"What happened?" he asked again.

I answered, "Your son met with an accident."

"How? When?"

I said, "I really don't know the details, he may be dead. But what I am concerned with is your wife—how she will take it. Please cooperate with me and help me."

He began to turn pale and he was given nitroglycerin and left with his daughter while I went upstairs.

I said to the wife, "I have some sad news for you, your son met with an accident. But what I am concerned with is your husband. You know that he has a serious heart condition, and the slightest exertion or emotion is liable to prove fatal. I want you to cooperate with me to save him."

"But what happened?"

Again I repeated, "Your son met with an accident. He may be dead. I don't know the details. But what I am concerned with is your husband. I want to save him, and I want to solicit your aid in cooperating with me." As I talked with her the husband came upstairs with his daughter.

With tears in his eyes he asked her, "How do you feel?"

"Never mind me," she replied, "how to you feel?"

Here, again, is a case which utilized the background of the patient; two five-year plans were drawn up to relieve the fear of imminent death by angina. Knowing the background and the devotion of the patients for each other, it was utilized in another emergency—in a sad tragedy which could have been made even worse.

Case III

The following case illustrates how utilizing the cultural background of the patient helped to overcome a hospital phobia in a patient who needed an emergency operation.

On the evening of March 21, 1932, I was called to see an elderly sick man on consultation—a man whose diagnosis was problematic.

Patient S.F., age seventy-six, whose chief complaint was abdominal pain of three days' duration. I felt that it was a case of acute appendicitis and urged an immediate operation.

As soon as the patient heard the word "operation" mentioned, he turned his head toward the wall and refused even to discuss the matter. He claimed that it was his wish to die in his own home, in his own bed. At that time his two little rooms were filled with his sons and daughters, his grandchildren and other relatives, each of them pleading with him to listen to the doctor's advice, but he refused.

As a last resort, I entered the room of the patient and speaking to the other members of the family, I said, "*Kibbud av*" (the first two words of the commandment, "Honor thy father"). "Honor thy father. Please don't argue with him. You must respect his wishes. If it is your father's will not to go to a hospital, you must respect his wish. Please leave the room and let me talk to him." Then I turned to the old man and said, "Grandfather, the hour is late and I must go; but first I wish to ask you to do me a favor. Tomorrow when they lower you into your grave and, according to Jewish lore, the angel will ask you your name, if perchance he should ask you to mention the names of those who contributed to the cause of your death, would you please do me the favor of telling the angel that it was not the fault of the physician. That according to the best of his ability he diagnosed the case and advised you to go to the hospital, but that you yourself refused to go. Goodbye and good luck."

"Just a moment," replied the patient.

But I said that I was sorry—that it was late and I must leave.

"Just one second," he pleaded, "I want to ask you—does a person die from this illness?"

"No," I replied, "if you carry out the advice of the physicians and surgeons. Otherwise it may prove fatal."

He then said to his wife, "Give me my *arba kanfot*" (fringed religious garment). And he went to the hospital.

He was admitted at 8:00 P.M. that evening and operated on the same night. A gangrenous appendix was removed. He made an uneventful recovery.

Here is a case where a patient born in Poland still retained the picture of the hospital in his native town—a dreadful place where patients were sent as a last resort, in terminal stages of their illness, and from which very few returned. By appealing to his deep religious background, which contained both law and lore, it was possible to break his resistance to his hospital phobia and proceed with modern medical treatment. As a matter of fact, one year later, on August 25, 1933, under localized anesthesia, a cataract was removed from his right eye and on December 9, 1935, a nucleation of the left cataract was performed.

Hospital records, no matter how complete in detail, lack the human element—as in this case, the fear of going to a hospital. However, without this human element there would have been no hospital record.

Case IV

The following case illustrates an even more perplexed complex—that of a broken-hearted mother who fixed the guilt of the death of her daughter on a physician, and the only way that she could be made to reason was by an appeal to a traditional Jewish ritual.

On one of New England's stormy winter days in February of 1933, I was called to see a man with an acute pharyngitis. Treatment was outlined to him and the man then said, "Will you please examine my wife as she is suffering from a heart attack."

Physical examination. Revealed a woman, aged fifty-six, with a moderate tachycardia; rate—120, heart was not enlarged, sounds were regular, no murmurs were heard; lungs—no rales; blood pressure 140/70; thyroid was not palpable, no exophthalmus present. Patient appeared tense and anxious. There were no signs or symptoms of hyperthyroidism. I prescribed triple-bromides and told her to take a dram TID. I reassured her that she had no heart trouble but that she was suffering from some emotional upset and that was the cause of her rapid heart action.

"Upset!" she exclaimed, "Why Doctor, my daughter was just

killed by a doctor!" Here she mentioned the name of a reputable Boston surgeon.

"What do you mean by that?" I asked, and she told me the following story:

Her daughter, age twenty-six had been stricken ten days previously with signs and symptoms of acute appendicitis. A surgeon was called in. He diagnosed the case correctly and took her to the hospital. She was operated on, and an acute inflamed appendix was removed. At the end of eight days she was brought home. A few hours later, while walking into her bedroom and looking over some gifts that had been sent to her, she dropped dead.

"Why, madam," I said, "the doctor did not kill your daughter. He did everything that was right and your daughter died of one of the complications that sometimes follow an operation."

She interrupted screaming, "You doctors," and jumped from her chair in a fit of hysteria. "You doctors have a union. You never talk against each other but you know very well in your heart that he killed her! If I had had Dr. ——, this thing would never have happened."

With this she collapsed in her chair, weeping.

I made several attempts to calm her, telling her that a similar episode had happened to the son of a state official whose death notice had recently appeared on the front page of all the Boston papers, but to no avail.

Again she said, "You doctors have a union, but you know the truth. That he killed her! Why didn't he kill me? I have lived my life! She was my source of joy and happiness!" Here she narrated, with tears in her eyes, the story of the life of her daughter, how she excelled in her studies, how beautiful she was, and with this she rushed out and brought in a picture of her. Then she described the funeral, etc.

Here is a mother whose heart was broken and bleeding over the premature death of her only daughter and she had fixed the guilt of death on the surgeon, who had done his duty and performed the operation. Any attempt to comfort her met with further association of me as a member of "the union" and thus a partner to the crime. I tried to counteract this by appealing to the cultural, religious background of the patient. I interrupted the conversation suddenly by saying to the woman, "Pardon me, but I forgot to ask your husband a very important question." I then said to the husband, "Do you wash your hands after going to the bathroom, according to the Jewish ritual law?"

"Yes," he replied.

Meanwhile, the woman remained with her mouth open, as if in the middle of a sentence, while tears were still flowing from her eyes.

I then said to the husband, "Do you recite the prayer *Asher Yazar* after you wash your hands?"

"To tell the truth," he said, "sometimes I do and sometimes I don't."

"Now," I said, "when you do recite it, do you know what it means?"

And he answered, "I must confess that I don't."

"Well," I said, "I shall recite the prayer for you, as it is one of the finest medical descriptions to be found anywhere."

"What does it mean?" he asked.

I started the recitation: "Blessed art Thou, O Lord our God, King of the universe, who has fashioned man in wisdom, and created in him many orifices and tubes. It is revealed and known before Thy glorious throne that if but one of these be opened or stopped, it would be impossible to exist and to stand before Thy presence. Blessed art Thou, O Lord, who healest all flesh and doest wondrously." As they both listened attentively I finished by saying, "One of those tubes closed—that is the cause of your daughter's death."

The husband turned to his wife and said, "Do you hear? The doctor is right. So it is written and it is the fault of no one."

Here I felt that my mission was performed and I had helped to sooth a mother's broken heart. I put on my coat and was about to leave when the woman turned to me and said, "Please, Doctor, cool off, you are sweating. It is cold and stormy outside. You may catch cold. We need you. You are a friend in need."

Discussion and Summary

By knowing well the cultural background of the patient, the physician can view the universe through the eyes of the patient.

He will then be able to understand the complexities of the texture and pattern of the patient's reasoning. A patient's actions and motivations become clear and understandable. A lack of understanding of the deep cultural background will often mislead a physician and cause him to draw a wrong conclusion, as illustrated by the following episode:

An elderly patient of mine, suffering from advanced Buerger's disease, was admitted to the hospital for amputation of the involved leg. I witnessed the operation, which was done under spinal anesthesia. In the tense, silent atmosphere of the operating room, as the surgeon was sawing the bone, the patient was heard mumbling in a chanting voice as if accompanying the rhythm of the saw. Whispering to the young resident anesthetist, I inquired about the patient's condition. He replied, "His pulse and blood pressure are good; but it seems as if the spinal anesthetic has affected his mind." I turned my ear to the patient and I heard him humming in Hebrew the words of an ancient prayer, "God, who performs miracles, who is the creator of medicine, etc." Does this indicate that the patient's mind was affected, or does it not point out that the young anesthetist was misled because of lack of knowledge of the patient's deep cultural background.

If we wish really to understand a patient's mode of thinking we must delve deeply into his history, culture, and tradition. In mental ailments, as in organic disease, we must understand the natural processes and work with them, not against them. This is true of all peoples and all nationalities. This is particularly true in the case of the Jew, who has a long history, a continuous culture, a vast literature, and an endless chain of traditions. All these factors modify the pattern of one's thinking. The reasoning processes are like long equations with several unknowns, where each symbol has to be worked out in order to solve the equations. Nor is there a slide-rule formula in medicine which would apply to all patients. Each one has to be studied individually and an estimate made of the entire personality.

Knowing the cultural background of the patient we can utilize it also as a therapeutic measure, for it permits the physician to penetrate into the very depths of the subconscious mind of the patient and bring it to the surface. The cultural background acts as a lever and will penetrate deep into the subconscious mind. The more the physician knows about the cultural background of the patient, the longer the arm of the lever is for lifting and bringing his point into the focus of the patient.

These four cases are not merely simple empirical incidents wherein the physician is called upon to give emotional support. The preservation and reproduction of the human voice or the recording electrocardiographically of electrical potentials of the heart muscle appear very simple superficially when once seen performed; but an analysis of these mechanical devices will reveal intricate basic scientific principles. So an analysis of these cases will reveal deep-rooted psychological problems and treatment scientifically based on an understanding of these problems.

Case I evolves around the deep-rooted Jewish psychology of *Kaddish,* a mourning prayer recited by a son after the departed parents. This prayer does not mention a word about death or the departed. It is merely a recital of the glorification of God. But so deeply rooted is this custom that to a Jew it means everything. In it he sees immortality. When he is gone his child—part of him—carries on his ideals. This psychology was briefly expressed by a wise Jew who was congratulated on his son's accomplishments in the academic world, whose fame was world-wide but who was not strict in his religious observances. He replied, *"Tzu a Kaddish kumt is nicht"* (Still he is not what is meant by a *Kaddish*).

In Case I the woman risked her life, in spite of the advice of her physicians, and gave birth to a son. Here is a deep subconscious motivation that prompted her to take the risk. The son was given a professional education at more sacrifice; and then he married out of his faith—which made him a lost cause. If he had died during the war, it would have been a death for the glory of the country and the flag. Psychologically there was death without glory, and instead of glory there was insult upon injury. To this mother it was a severe psychic trauma which revealed itself in the various somatic manifestations. This problem was brought to the surface, but it was difficult to integrate it in her conscious mind and to make her see that he was still alive and still part of her. Her rational processes were blocked by intense emotions. One could not reason with her. She would not listen to reason. In order to focus her attention, it was decided to tell her an innocent story—a kind of psychological detour as an approach to the very core of her rational processes—a superficially innocent story in which a great rabbi, who in the eyes of the religious Jew is final authority in questions of law, plays the main role. In the rabbi's case his own daughter leaves him and his environment when she grows up. The story also reveals a man who, though converted, is not considered a total loss by the rabbi. If such a man asks for mercy he still has a chance.

The second case deals with a keen businessman who becomes the victim of a very serious ailment, angina of effort. He is retired from his busy daily routine and every day reads the trends in the stock market quotations as well as the death column. One cause of death he understands—so-and-so died of heart attack. Death stares at him, and he develops an intense fear of it until it finally becomes an obsession with him. This is not calm resignation to it. The fear is so intense that all words of encouragement rebound. The road to intellectual insight is blocked by fear. Therefore, an approach is made again by way of a detour—sidetracking his illness by focusing his mind on the romance of Palestine. The rejuvenation of a people is portrayed—the drama of Israel for many centuries. It is a fascinating story to listen to. While still absorbed in the story a suggestion is made to him, that in five years he should go to Palestine and see this drama staged before his own eyes. He swallowed a smooth pill without effort. The pill was further sugar-coated by appealing to his devotion to his wife, as such an experience would appeal to her religious instincts. As time goes on and nothing happens to him, his fear lessens and he has a goal, a five-year plan.

To lessen the emotional shock of the sudden death of a son to a person suffering from angina pectoris, another procedure was used. The tragedy of the accident was somewhat sidetracked by an appeal to him to cooperate in saving his wife, to whom he was devoted. She, on the other hand, was taken into confidence to spare the life of her husband. To further dampen the tragic jolt, I advised the family to have the funeral in the West and the temporary burial there. Meanwhile, the father would fulfill his duties by merely reciting the *Kaddish* at home on the day of the funeral. Such was the case.

The third case illustrates an old Jew whose mental picture of an old Polish hospital made him dread all hospitals and close his eyes and ears to any suggestion about going to the hospital, no matter how urgent the case might be. Fear blocked the pathway to intellectual insight. It was opened by a back door. By telling the family to respect his decisions no matter what they might be, as it is the duty of children to respect their parents, I gained his confidence and made him feel that the physician was an ally to his cause. I then asked him to do me a favor and tell the "angel" that the doctor had done his duty and so the cause of death, if and when it came, would be his own. This is not merely frightening a patient with death, for his fear of hospitals was even greater; but it has a more profound appeal. The religious Jew is taught that to preserve his own life is as sacred as saving the lives of others. Committing suicide is looked upon as a mortal sin and such a person is buried near the wall of the cemetery. Thus, the dreadful mental pictures associated with hospitals vanished from his mind, and he listened to advice.

The last case illustrates a mother who lost her only daughter because of a postoperative accident and focuses the guilt on the innocent surgeon. Attempts to explain this accident merely made the physician a partner to the guilt, one who belonged to the same "union." She felt that the physician knew the facts as she imagined them to be, but that he was merely concealing them. An iron curtain blocks all appeals to reason. Intellectual insight is gained by a sudden interruption of the discussion by the recital of an innocent prayer, one which is repeated daily in the Orthodox mode of living. This prayer made clear to her the logic of embolic phenomena. The authors of prayers cannot be accused of "union" membership. Psychologically there is, indeed, power in prayer.

To conclude, these four cases serve as a reminder of a definite law about human mental behavior. Just as on the physical side, in order to understand the functions of an organ, we study its evolutionary development, embryology as well as the anatomical and microscopic studies, so in the mental pattern of a patient we must not only delve into the complete history of a person but into the cultural background of the particular race from which he sprung. Every person carries within him mental seeds of culture from numerous generations that anteceded him. In the words of a noted poet and psychologist,

> Our deeds still travel with us from afar,
> And what we have been makes us what we are.

Summary

An attempt is made in this paper to show how significant it is for the physician to know the cultural background of the patient in order to diagnose and treat certain beliefs and traditions which are deeply rooted in the cultural history of a people. When these beliefs are challenged, in some instances psychosomatic problems develop. These four cases deal with Jewish patients whose people have a long, continuous cultural history, with traditions and beliefs going back for many centuries. In such cases it is well that the physician himself be acquainted and familiar with the evolution of those ideas. In this way he can reveal their complexities and bring their problems to the surface.

Not only will a knowledge of the cultural background of the patient help in the diagnosis of the disease, but it can also be made to act as a therapeutic agent.

This article appeared also in *Studies in Motivation* by David C. McClelland, ed. (Appleton-Century-Crofts, New York, 1975).

The Dream as a Diagnostic Aid in Physical Diagnosis

Dreams are the true interpreters of our inclinations, but art is required to sort and understand them.

—Montaigne

These whimsical pictures, inasmuch as they originate from us, may well have an analogy with our whole life and fate.

—Goethe

The interpretation of dreams is the royal road to our knowledge of these unconscious activities of the mind.

—Freud

Freud, Jung, Adler, and their disciples have succeeded, in a measure, in deciphering the ephemeral, mystical language of the dream. Freud, for the first time, formulated the actual science of dream interpretation as an integral part of the psychoanalytic method. He and others have postulated that the dream protects the dreamer from awakening, and that outside events may be incorporated into the dream. But according to Freud's discussion, the mechanism of the dream consists of processes by which mental conflicts, wishes, anxieties, or other

First published in *Connecticut Medicine,* May 1969.

states find expression during sleep. The function of the dream is to disguise and distort in order to allow the continuance of sleep. In psychoanalysis these conflicts are traced back to an early or even an infantile period of life and later revived and brought into prominence in the consciousness of the dreamer.

The unraveling and interpretation of these complex situations lies in the province of the analyst. There are, however, instances in the experience of the internist in which patients will reveal a dream involving a comparatively recent experience that is dramatized or symbolized in a manner not too complicated to lend itself to interpretation. There may be an external physical stimulus that disturbs the sleeping person, but the dream will disguise it so as not to awaken him. This may be illustrated by a situation in which a student retiring very late sets his clock to awaken him at an early hour for his class. But as the alarm clock rings, he dreams that it is Sunday and he is hearing the church bells chime and he continues to sleep undisturbed; or there may be an internal and somewhat painful experience that might interrupt his sleep and the dreamer again dramatizes the episode in a manner that permits him to sleep. Not every dream is so intricate or complicated that elaborate analysis is required.

In the search for a proper diagnosis, one may find the dream to be a diagnostic aid. The dream may direct us to the vital organs that are involved in the symptoms of the patient, so that the physician may concentrate his search in that area; or if the physical examination is essentially negative, the dream may help to explain the patient's signs and symptoms of psychic origin.

The dreams in the following cases bear witness to Freud's comment that the function of the dream is to protect the sleeper from being disturbed by stimuli that otherwise might awaken him. This is accomplished by a process of distortion whereby the real meaning of the dream is disguised from the dreamer; a dual process which Freud calls plastic representation, including symbolism and dramatization. The images of the dream are symbols which use the subconscious thought of the dreamer.

Now in medical diagnosis, as in sleuthing in crime detection, every bit of evidence is helpful in determining the cause of a person's ailment. In the following situations the dreams of the patients were used as aids in diagnosing the illness.

A young man, thirty-six years old, white, unmarried, came into my office complaining of an occasional fluttery feeling in his stomach. In every other respect he felt perfectly well; he had just returned from a vacation in Bermuda. The evening before, while driving his car, he became aware of this fluttery sensation. He said that he had not wished to disturb me that night and had consulted a neighborhood physician who prescribed a tranquilizer for him. He slept well that night except for a disturbing dream. He dreamt that he fell from a wharf in Bermuda and landed in the water between the wharf piles and a yacht that was moored alongside. The motion of the yacht squeezed him against the structure of the pier.

The resulting physical examination was essentially negative and on the surface did not indicate further study. But the vivid recollection of the details of his dream which had so disturbed him did concern me, and made me suspicious that they might have been due to some precoronary discomfort. I took an electrocardiogram and noted ST segment and T wave changes, suggestive of an acute myocardial infarction. He was referred to the hospital; diagnosis was confirmed and he was treated with coronary precautions. He made an uneventful recovery. I feel that in this case his dream was a clue that pointed to a coronary attack. In his sleep he was experiencing the painful symptoms of acute coronary insufficiency, and the dream protected him from awakening.

On the other hand, the following situation demonstrates the dream as an aid to diagnosis in reverse—contrary to the patient's complaints of symptoms that he felt were due to damage to his heart, the dream pointed to a diagnosis of psychosomatic origin.

A man, sixty years of age, a lawyer by profession, came to the office with complaints of palpitation, fatigue, nervousness, and fear that in his sleep he had suffered a "heart attack." The following is a digest of his story. He had been perfectly well the day before, pursued his daily routine with no sense of dyspnea or precardial distress. That night he went to bed at his usual hour, but later recalled that he had a dreadful dream that disturbed him, and on awakening he was trembling, his heart was "beating like a drum"—he had a sweat and was shivering with fear, believing that he had suffered a heart attack.

His physical examination was essentially negative; there was no change in his normal blood pressure of 130/70; his pulse was 64. An electrocardiogram was taken which was normal in all respects, and showed no changes from one taken previously in a routine physical checkup. Since there were no somatic signs to explain his symptoms, the details of his very disturbing dream were gone into thoroughly. Perhaps they would yield a clue to a psychic origin, and the following is a rather detailed report of his dream.

He was walking with his chief along a main thoroughfare in front of a large office building when he suddenly became paralyzed and could not walk any farther. This dreadful episode caused him to awake from a deep sleep with great fear. Upon further questioning, he disclosed a number of important facts— the office building in front of which he was walking was the location of the office wherein he was employed. The patient was a graduate of a leading law school and had an M.A. degree. He was well thought of by the members of the firm in which he was employed; he had received small raises in salary from time to time, but his main duties continued to be routine, and he had not advanced to partnership in the firm. His chief, on the other hand, with only a A.B. degree, had been pushed ahead as the firm grew, and his salary had jumped accordingly.

From my knowledge and observations of this patient through the years, I felt that he was, although obviously a good student of the law, inarticulate and lacked other qualities necessary for spectacular success in this field.

After some preliminary discussion, he was asked point-blank, "Haven't you ever thought that in spite of having a higher degree than your chief you have not achieved his position nor his financial rewards?" He answered, "I have often thought that but kept these thoughts to myself." After some further discussion he began to accept the fact that scholarship alone could not bring him the results he desired.

I felt this situation was indicated in the dream in which he became "paralyzed" as he walked with his chief. He was assured of his good physical condition and that in my opinion there was no heart involvement to account for his symptoms. After some consideration of my interpretation of the sign of his distress, he seemed to find the explanation satisfactory and has continued to be in essentially good condition.

Summary

The two cases reported demonstrate that the dream can be an important aid in physical diagnosis—it can serve as a clue leading to the etiology of the patient's ailment. Verily did an ancient rabbi say, "A dream not interpreted is like a letter unread" (Rabbi Ḥisda, *Berakhot* 55a).

Psycho-Paracentesis in Internal Medicine: Study of Six Cases

The first duty of the internist on seeing the patient is to diagnose the illness and then to treat it. After a complete and thorough history and physical examination, those cases which require specialized care are referred to the various specialists. The office of the internist is, in a sense, a screening place for patients. On the other hand, a patient who requires a minor surgical procedure is usually taken care of by the physician himself, for as long as he understands the principles of asepsis and surgical technic, he feels he is well equipped to do this rather than refer the patient to a surgeon. In most instances it is of benefit to the patient, as well as to the physician.

It seems that this is equally true of psychic disorders. Cases of major, complicated psychiatric problems are referred to specialists who will use specific therapy, such as psychoanalysis, shock treatments, or lobotomy. However, not every problem requires a prolonged psychoanalysis or shock treatment. There are not enough psychiatrists to treat all the minor mental problems. Using again the analogy of organic disease, if a physician finds a patient suffering from a superficial abscess that is walled-off, he is well equipped to handle the situation by

First published in *American Practitioner and Digest of Treatment,* June 1954.

merely an incision and drainage. I use the term "walled-off" advisedly, for nature has built up a wall in order to prevent the spread of infection, and it is better to do as little surgery as possible so as not to break this protecting wall. Similarly, in mental complaints it is often advisable to localize and bring to the surface a complex that disturbs the patient and which is responsible for his particular symptoms, thus giving him relief rather than delving, probing, and disturbing complexes that bear no relation to the present illness, and which by suggestion may even cause new disturbances. The method used in the following cases is brief and simple, and I prefer to call it by the name of *psycho-paràcentesis,* that is, puncturing the psychic complex. Just as the physician trained in surgical technic merely incises and drains the "walled-off" abscess, so the physician trained in the principles of psychology brings the mental problem to the surface and the tension is thus relieved. Further probing is often unnecessary. Of course the physician must know the various theories and principles of psychology, normal as well as abnormal, and utilize the contributions of the various schools of psychology. This method guards us against the fallacy of the Middle Ages, when every case was treated according to the teachings of Galen. We in medicine must utilize the contributions of every school of medicine and every form of therapy as long as it helps the patient, just as we make use of chemical compounds developed by the chemist and isotopes developed by the atomic physicist.

The following six cases illustrate the procedure of psychoparacentesis. It is not a short form of psychoanalysis even though it uses some Freudian concepts; there is no transference, nor does sex, even in the Freudian sense, play a major part. Each case is dealt with individually to release the tension that brought about the symptoms, as if it were a mental abscess that has to be evacuated. In other words, this is not merely a form of differentiation between psychosomatic disease and organic disease, but more than that; it is a form of therapy in which the key is found to the riddle that produces the symptoms. These cases may appear simple once the mechanism is revealed, but like a puzzle, once we know how to do it it is quite simple.

Case I

Mrs. M.K. came into my office stating that five days previously she had entered a bank to transact some business and while standing at the teller's cage she felt dizzy, fainted, and fell to the floor, hitting her head and elbow. Unconsciousness lasted for a few minutes. There was no loss of control of sphincters and no frothing from the mouth. After a short time she was able to drive home. There was no history of tarry stools and no signs of internal hemorrhage.

Physical examination. Essentially negative. Blood pressure was 115/70 and pulse was 80. Her past history was irrelevant. She is married and has two sons living and well.

Here was a case of syncope with no indications of any organic etiology. The patient was questioned further in search of some psychogenic mechanism for this attack of syncope. On further questioning as to the minute details of what went through her mind during the business transaction, the following information was obtained: She entered the bank for the purpose of cashing certain shares which had matured. They were in her son's name, as well as her own, and she was wondering if her son's signature was necessary or not when the fainting spell came on. Further questioning brought out the fact that several years ago she had been arrested for petty larceny, for which she had been sent to a reformatory for fourteen months; now she felt that should this be revealed, it might prove injurious to her childrens' reputations.

It was explained to this patient that here was a case in which the mere signing of her signature brought back the unpleasant suppressed experience, and this was sufficient to cause syncope.

Discussion. Here is a case in which syncope was produced by the association of an act with a previous sad experience which probably had been suppressed. There is no transference, and by a simple method of association of her acts with the previous experience, the entire situation was brought to the surface. Here the physician acted in a sense as a "father confessor," and the mere revealing of the story acted as a form of catharsis and released the unpleasant experience which had acted as a foreign body.

Case II

Mrs. N.F., age twenty-five, came into my office with her chief
complaint of inability to swallow food, which began four months
previously. She stated that she had difficulty in taking liquids as
well as solids. Food caused her to gag and was followed by
belching. She claimed that during the last four months she had
lost 17 pounds. She did not recall anything that might have
precipitated this condition. As a matter of fact, at that time they
had just moved into a newly-purchased home and were very
happy and contented. She had been to other physicians in her
home state and was given some drug to take which she claims
made her mouth dry but did not help her (probably atropine).
She had a complete G.I. series and fluoroscopy, with negative
findings. Her past history revealed that she was always well
except for the usual childhood diseases, including tonsillectomy
and adenoidectomy. She had been very happily married for
three years; she had no children. Her father died of a blood clot
at the age of forty-seven, and her mother died five years
previously, of essential hypertension, at the age of forty-two. She
has one brother living and well.

Physical examination. Essentially negative. Her weight was
121½ pounds; her usual weight was about 137 pounds. Pulse was
72; BP, 120/80. Further questioning revealed no particular
worries. She stated that nothing was upsetting her.

Since this episode began with her moving into the new house, I
felt that the present illness was in some way associated with it.
Furthermore, since various physical examinations, including the
present one, plus roentgenologic examination, revealed no
organic disease, this disorder must have had a psychosomatic
origin. She had every reason to be happy. A detailed questioning
of every minute incident, beginning with the buying of the
house, was started. It was found that when they moved to this
new home a neighbor, a man whom she did not know, passed
away. She did not know any of the details concerning his death,
nor did the neighbor's death upset her in any way. She was asked
if the death of her neighbor brought to mind any similar episode
in her family. The patient was then asked whether she felt that
she would have liked to have had her mother share her new

home and happiness with her. That question filled the patient's eyes with tears, and she replied that it was so. She was asked to tell, in detail, her thoughts on this matter, and she stated that one day, while making beds, she had thought about it but brushed it aside. The incident of the neighbor's death probably brought it more vividly to her mind. She was told that remembering her mother was a noble thought, but that brushing it aside was futile; it should not be done. I explained that one does not dismiss things from one's mind so easily; one merely suppresses them and they reveal themselves in various symptoms. She was told to think about it and always to remember her mother and to try to do something which would perpetuate her memory. She was reasured that once she realized the situation, the symptoms would disappear.

A tonic with some sedation was precribed to be taken before meals, and tablets of Syntropan were to be taken after meals if she had any belching. Since her home was out of the state she was asked to remain in Boston a few more days in order that I might see whether this procedure had worked. She was also told to report any dreams that she might have.

She returned three days later to report that she did not find it necessary to take the tablets after meals, as there was no distress. Physical examination revealed that she had gained three and one-half pounds; pulse was 76; BP, 110/90. She was cheerful and happy. She related the following dream: Several people were invited to a party and after preparing a salad which consisted of vegetables and eggs, to her great surprise there was not enough food for everyone there, especially for the hostess with whom she was staying. She exclaimed, "What am I going to do now? There is not enough . . . !" and the dream ended. On further questioning it was learned that after her mother's death she had stayed with a grandmother, who did all the cooking. She was very grateful to her grandmother, and she felt very sorry that she had never had the opportunity to return the kindness in her own home. Her dream was interpreted in this manner: her happiness was incomplete because she did not have the people she wanted most with her, and with whom she might enjoy her happiness, and this was the reversal of having them and not having enough food for them. She left for her hometown, reassured and perfectly well. She was asked to communicate with me in regard to future developments.

Three days later the patient's brother came in to see me regarding his own health and gave more information about his sister. They had been brought up in a family of meager means, and conditions were such that there was just enough money to pay the rent and buy food; at times she was able to go to a movie with a friend. She was the only daughter, and spoiled. As he put it, "She was a little brat. Everyone catered to her. Now she is married to a person whose income is more than sufficient, and she feels rather sorry for the way she acted and would like to repay." The story the brother told corroborated the previous solution of the case.

Discussion. Here we have a much more complicated case in which a young woman developed dysphagia, and by the method of psycho-paracentesis we not only penetrated the immediate problem, but release was obtained by acquainting the patient with the facts and by my suggesting to her that she repay her debts in some other way. Like an incision of a "walled-off" abscess, she was relieved of her symptoms. By association of every minute detail, when these symptoms became revealed and in spite of her outer happiness, it was found that she suffered with a guilty conscience. Her cruel attitude toward her poor parents in her youth, particularly to her mother, who had made every sacrifice in order to please her whims and fancies, could not be assuaged. Now that she was in a position to repay them in some measure, she found that it was too late; the parents were gone. She developed dysphagia, a form of self-punishment. Again, by merely penetrating the immediate problem, release was obtained and the patient was relieved of her symptoms.

It is also of interest to note that in her dream she prepared a salad of eggs and vegetables. In Jewish lore eggs are usually eaten by mourners, for the egg is a symbol of the life-cycle, i.e., every person is born and is destined to die. Also, on the most joyous festival, for example, the celebration of Jewish independence, Passover eve, an egg is placed on the table, for even in great joy one must also keep in mind that the final goal of man in life is the grave.

Case III

Miss S.G., age thirty, was sent to me by a physician for an evaluation of her cardiac condition. Her chief complaint was shortness of breath, although she was able to walk for some distance without distress. She also complained of other bizarre symptoms: a feeling of nausea and an uncomfortable, choked feeling. This had started a few months before when her brother returned from the Pacific war area and told her of his horrible experiences during the war.

Her past history was irrelevant. She had the usual childhood diseases, and one year before she had been operated on for an ovarian cyst by the same surgeon who had referred her to me. Her father was living and well. Her mother had died during the influenza epidemic at the age of thirty-two. She had one brother and two sisters living and well.

She claimed that during the last few days she had to "sigh for breath" every few minutes, and this was accompanied by headaches. (On watching her, I found that she did take a deep sigh every few minutes. It, however, was not actual dyspnea.) There was no loss of weight or any other complaints. Her periods were regular and of normal duration; there was no dysmenorrhea.

Physical examination. Essentially negative, except for frequent deep breaths, as if she were sighing. Her heart was negative; there were no murmurs. The heart rate was 80; BP, 100/70. Patient was asked to exercise for a few minutes, and it was noted that the pulse rate went up to 96 and then came back to normal within two minutes.

Since organic heart disease was ruled out, it was felt that her symptoms were of psychogenic origin. She was then asked to tell of any dreams she might have had, and she replied that she had recurrent dreams of someone being killed by an automobile. She explained this dream as being due to the fact that one of her sisters had been killed in an automobile accident. She was then told that there might be a much deeper reason for the dream. She refused to accept this, insisting that her sister was killed in this manner, which was true, and that alone explained the contents of the dream.

We temporarily dismissed the discussion of the dream and

went on to further questioning. It was revealed that she was in love with a young man. When asked if she was going to marry him, she claimed that she couldn't marry him because he had an older sister who had complete possession of him. I told her that this should not be a serious obstacle, for after her marriage she would be the one who would possess him. At this point she exclaimed, "But I can't marry him. Very frequently he spits up blood. He had rheumatic fever and as a result he was left with serious heart trouble, and he frequently gets very ill."

The patient was told that if she really loved him, she alone must make the decision. She then exclaimed, "Suppose he dies! I would have no one. I have no mother, and I would be left completely alone." Here the patient was questioned, "Did it ever occur to you that the man you see killed in your dream resembles your boy friend?"

All through this conversation about the dream and her love affair the patient was absorbed and had ceased sighing. The patient was made aware of the fact that throughout the conversation, which lasted about an hour, her difficulty in breathing seemed to have subsided and that her symptoms were merely subconscious emulations of her boy friend's illness and not a result of any organic cardiac condition.

Discussion. This case reveals a cardiac neurosis which came about as a result of the fear of marrying a person who was suffering from a serious cardiac disorder which threatened his life; subconsciously the patient expressed that fear by emulating cardiac symptoms. Here, by utilization of the dream and careful history, it was possible to puncture this complex and bring the whole problem to the surface, which alleviated the patient's symptoms.

Case IV

I was called to see a young girl, age fourteen, who was complaining of abdominal pain starting at the umbilical region and radiating to the right side. Pain was intermittent.

Physical examination. Revealed a well-developed, well-nourished young girl lying in bed weeping. She had been perfectly well that day and toward evening she got this attack.

She had had a similar episode during the summer while staying at a girls' camp. The physical examination at the present time was essentially negative. Her abdomen was soft; there was no spasm or tenderness. Temperature was normal. During the entire examination it was noted that the patient acted as though she were a third party to the whole situation.

Since she showed no concern during the entire physical examination, and since the examination was negative, an attempt was made to probe into her emotional life. It was revealed that she was a refugee who had come from Europe two years previously. Her mother and sister had been murdered in a German concentration camp. She had come to America with her father. She then stated that her father was about to remarry. With tears in her eyes she asserted that she was not against it—that she wanted him to remarry; however, she felt the pain of the loss of her mother.

This physical manifestation of abdominal pain was merely a reflection of her mental state.

Discussion. Here is a case of abdominal pain which came on as a result of mental agony due to the fact that her father was to remarry and some strange woman would take her mother's place. Outwardly, however, she consented to her father's remarrying so that he would not have to live alone. Being unable to reconcile these two opposite loyalties, her anguish manifested itself in abdominal pain. In other words, her abdomen was uttering a protest. Just as the recti muscles become rigid and tender, reflecting an organic disease, so symptoms of the abdomen may reveal the reflections of mental agony. Once the appendix is removed the muscles relax; so in removing the mental pain the abdominal symptoms disappear. This young woman's problem was analyzed, the peculiar situation of her father was explained, and her symptoms were relieved.

Case V

Mr. K.T. consulted me in 1947 for cramplike discomfort in the stomach and frequent bowel movements of several years' duration. This had begun some time ago with a generalized discomfort throughout the abdomen. He had consulted several physicians regarding this in his home state. A roentgenograph was taken and he was fluoroscoped on at least two occasions, but the findings were negative. The stools were cultured and were found to be negative also. He was careful in choosing his diet, claiming that some foods "pass right through" him—no one food in particular; however, his diet was adequate. He took multivitamins three times a day.

His past history revealed that he had always been well. In 1922 he had his appendix removed. He has been married for twenty-four years and had one son, eighteen years of age, living and well.

Family history. Revealed that his father had died of asthma at the age of sixty-two and his mother had died at the age of forty-six, cause unknown. He had three brothers and three sisters living and well. The rest of the systemic history is essentially negative. His average weight was about 155 pounds. He denied having any worries and claimed that he had no fears. His marital life was perfectly happy. He had a grammar school education, but was forced to begin working at an early age in order to support himself.

Physical examination. Revealed a well-developed and moderately well nourished man; his weight was 148½ pounds. The remainder of the examination was essentially negative. After the examination the patient asked how his tonsils were, and I told him that they were small, atrophied, and showed no signs of infection. I also noted that the patient wore a truss. When he was questioned about it he said that after his appendectomy in 1922, he was told that if he didn't wear a belt he might develop a hernia; however, the examination revealed no signs of a hernia. The fact that he wore the truss to prevent developing a hernia revealed the personality of the patient; he was subject to fear and was hyper-suggestive.

The patient was told to dress, but not to put the truss on. He was then called back into my office for further interrogation. "Why did you ask me about your tonsils?" he was asked.

He replied, "That's peculiar. . . . When I was a child in the second grade, the school physician examined my throat and told me that my tonsils were enlarged and infected, and that I should tell my mother to have them removed. But I never did tell her."

He was then asked to recall other episodes from his early childhood.

"That's strange," he remarked, "no physician has ever asked such questions before. But since you mention it, I do recall that at the age of five I went down into our cellar, where a passageway connected with the neighboring house, and there I found an open can of condensed milk. I drank most of the contents, and then I happened to spill a little of the milk on my hand and found that it was filled with ants. I never told anyone of this episode."

Here the patient was given my impression of his case; starting with the tonsils as an illustration, I pointed out that he was a person beset with all kinds of fears and phobias. The fact that his tonsils had not been removed was a good thing, as they did not require removal; but the fact that he did not transmit the school physician's message to his mother was still preying on his mind; unconsciously he feared that the infection was spreading throughout his system. At this point he was reassured and told that there was nothing to fear.

The episode concerning the condensed milk which he drank and which was contaminated with ants also contributed to his present illness. Subconsciously he believed that colonies of ants were still inhabiting his gastro-intestinal tract. He was again reassured that the ants, if he had swallowed any, had long ago been destroyed and would have had no ill effect on him. It was further explained to him that his insistence on wearing a belt because of someone's slight suggestion that he might develop a hernia revealed the type of personality he was. He was given the following directions: (1) stop all medication; (2) eat everything or anything that he might desire without any hesitation; (3) stop wearing the truss. I also told him that I was confident that from this time on he would be well, and asked him to write and inform me of his condition in about a week.

Two weeks later he informed me:

I believe that the two weeks just passed since my visit to you were the most trouble-free I have had for a long time. I am very happy about the whole thing. I am sticking rigidly to your advice. . . . I saw the truss you wanted me to destroy for the first time today and that was when we repacked our luggage. I left it home with no fear whatsoever. . . . I want to express my appreciation for the length of time you devoted to my visit, also for the consequences thereof.

Six months later the following correspondence was received from the wife of this man, and I believe it speaks for itself:

So you haven't heard the last of us! You see I was just testing—wanted to be sure your miraculous cure was not a temporary thing. After over — years of what surely seemed a chronic disorder of the intestinal and disgestive tract, with all its accompanying discomforts, the living with the proof of what you've done, it still seems unbelievable. . . . It's over six months since his visit to you so I really feel he's been "cured" by your amazing approach and understanding.

Discussion. This case is somewhat more complicated and more chronic, and has continued for a numer of years. It started with a suppressed fear in his childhood when a physician told him to go home and tell his mother to have his tonsils removed, as they poured pus into his system. This demonstrates how great is the power of words. Words are like magic bullets; they can either cure or injure. A physician must always guard himself against making rash statements to a patient. The second psychic trauma came about when he drank condensed milk in which he found ants. The treatments of subsequent physicians merely perpetuated his phobia, which was focused in the gastro-intestinal tract. A physician, then, must also guard himself against accentuating a patient's symptoms. Tests should be done to rule out organic disease, but once reassured of no abnormalities, the physician should focus his attention on the mental origin of the disease and not merely dismiss the complaint with the phrase, "There is nothing wrong with you!" or inform the patient that it is all mental. As seen in this case, these two episodes were uncovered by a thorough investigation of his childhood experiences, and once the patient was aware of them his symptoms disappeared. Here is a case where a gastric neurosis was worked out during one session.

Case VI

Mrs. F.G., age thirty-four, consulted me in 1939. Her chief complaint was nervousness, recurring backpain, insomnia, and loss of appetite. She felt fatigued and stated that she felt as if she were dying. These symptoms had begun about five months before. She had been to several physicians and amphetamine was prescribed, which made her even more nervous.

Past history. She was born in Russia and came to the United States at the age of two. She received a grammar school and high school education.

Family history. The father was living and well; the mother died of heart trouble when patient was an infant. Her father then married her mother's sister, and had four children by his second wife. Her stepmother did not treat her well. She claims that she was treated as though they did not want her. Later her father and stepmother separated.

She had been married three years. She had one miscarriage and then had one child, which was now about two years old. Her marital life seemed to be satisfactory. The patient could not explain any cause or source of worry; further response to questioning was unsatisfactory. She was then asked to recall any dreams she might had had, and her reply was that she didn't recall any dream in particular. She was then given a pad of paper and left in the consultation room, and told to concentrate and try to recall any dreams that she might have had. She recorded the following: She dreamt that there was an opening in a wall for a dumb-elevator, and in the dream she saw her baby fall into the open elevator shaft. She said, "I screamed, 'My baby!' I thought he was dead; but as I looked into the shaft I saw that the elevator was at a level with the floor and my child was unhurt. With this I woke up feeling restless and exhausted—as though I had been 'put through a wringer!' "

This dream seemed to be a clue to the situation, and I asked her to recall any other incident—whether dream or reality—which involved her child.

She finally revealed the following episode: After she had seen several physicians without obtaining any relief from her symptoms, one physician told her to take a vacation. Since the train made a stop at the New York terminal, she left the baby in his berth and went out on the platform to converse with a friend whom she had met by previous arrangement. As she was absorbed in conversation a conductor passed and she asked him, "When does the train leave for Pittsburgh?"

The conductor replied, "Madam, your train is pulling out now!"

"I screamed," she said " 'My baby!' And with these words I jumped onto the slowly-moving train."

Three hours of consultation, the dream, and this episode clarified the situation. I said to the woman, "Madam, it sccms to me that your baby stands in your way and you would like to get rid of him, and that is what your story and dream mean to me."

At these words the patient jumped from her chair, raised her arms in protest, and shouted, "How dare you say that to me! I love my baby! I am his mother!" With these words she burst into tears.

I calmed her down and explained to her that of course she loved her child—otherwise she would have done away with him, and this was the conflict in her mind, because she was not a "good sport."

"What do you mean by that?" she asked.

To which I replied, "Madam, if you want something that is very dear to you, you must sacrifice something else for it. Here is an illustration. I spent over three hours with you. You could not afford to pay for all the time I have given you nor would I ask you to. I have given you my time and effort, but in return I have learned something. As for you, when you wish a child, you must give up other things in life because of the child. For example, you cannot go out and attend various social and communal organizations as you did before the child was born. Now the child keeps you confined at home—but it is worth it. That is what I mean by being a 'sport.' "

The patient was given a simple tonic and was told that now that she understood the situation, I felt confident that her symptoms would leave her, which they did.

The following is a letter which I received from her husband on May 1, 1939.

My thanks to you for the kind consideration and patience you showed Mrs. F. on our visit to your office. During the past week she has responded quite well and I am keeping my fingers crossed. Her sleep is greatly improved and her attitude has also changed for the better. She let herself go a week ago Sunday, but since then it has been very pleasant. Everyone about her seems to note the improvement, but is not saying a word and are permitting her to go on as if nothing had happened.

Discussion. This is the most complicated case, and yet it was solved during one afternoon session although it took over three hours. Here is a neurosis which developed in a home as a result of a child interfering with the mother's activities. It had reached such a state that the mother subconsciously wanted to rid herself of the baby, but being a mother she did not dare think of it. Interpretation of the dream and other episodes was able to bring it to the surface. Here was a psycho-paracentesis that was painful, and the patient resented the physician when the facts were brought out; psychoanalysts might say that this patient had a psychoneurotic behavior which probably would require deep analysis, but once her symptoms were relieved there was no need to go further. Who knows whether a thorough psychoanalysis would be wise? It might stir up a lot of other emotions which might even make the patient worse.

Summary

The above six cases illustrate the method of psycho-paracentesis as it can be used in the office of the internist. It is not a brief psychoanalysis, nor is it a mere form of catharsis, but rather a method by which the symptoms of the patients are traced to their mental origin, and in this way the patients are relieved of their symptoms. It is a procedure by which diagnosis, as well as treatment, is done at the same time. It is as if these people were suffering from a mental abscess which the physician incised and drained. After all, was not the father of psychoanalysis, Josef Breuer, a great Viennese general practitioner? For it is he who recognized that many patients suffering from certain types of neurosis could be cured simply by getting them to talk and recall painful episodes of their earlier life. It was Breuer who sowed the seeds from which psychoanalysis grew. No physical examination is complete without some essential laboratory work as well as psychological probing, which every good physician ought to be equipped to do. The family physician, who knows the patient well, is best equipped to treat such cases, rather than relegate them all to the psychiatrist.

Part IV
Miscellany

The Physician and Prayer

The World Medical Association recently proposed a revision of the Hippocratic Oath. The association seems to feel that the original oath is archaic in form and content—for example, the invocation of Apollo and Aesculapius. Perhaps a new oath will bring it more up to date. But it is not the oath or its contents that is at fault. Rather it is we who are at fault, to whom prayer has lost its zest. Prayer has lost its spiritually uplifting flavor for us, and we jest about it. The most appetizing food will not appeal to an acutely ill patient suffering from fever, nausea, and general malaise.

Under normal conditions, when men strove for ethical standards and the air was permeated with religious feelings, the Hippocratic Oath served its purpose well. Whoever the author of the Hippocratic Oath was, he must have been a genius, for the oath expresses the high ideals of the merciful calling of medicine. It portrays the duties of a physician. It is no wonder that for two thousand years Jews, Christians, and Moslems have recited the oath upon completing their medical training. What is more important, however, is the emotion that people must have experienced in reciting the oath. But nowadays, since we do not believe in oaths, we miss that emotional experience. This is merely a symptom of the situation in the world at large at the present time. We are living in a world of anxiety, and we feel that

First published in *Journal of Pastoral Care,* Spring 1961.

the pillars upon which our entire civilization rests are crumbling. Dr. D. Elton Trueblood outlines the thought that the most grievous of man's ills is the failure of his spiritual growth to parallel his technical progress. In other words, there is a disparity between man's secular and ethical development. According to Trueblood, we have based our progress on "power culture." "The essential notion of power culture is the effort to organize human life independent of moral inhibition."[1]

In medical education, too, we suffer from the same ailment. Medicine has developed in the last fifty years by leaps and bounds. New fields of research have been discovered; new weapons to fight disease: magic drugs, chemotherapy, and antibiotics; new instruments which have expanded the human power of detection and observation—the electrocardiograph, x-ray, and radioactive isotopes. But what about the physician himself? All these discoveries and new drugs have given the physician more power; now he is better equipped to fight disease. But what about the man himself?

Harvey, if he could come back to us at this time, would be at a loss to read electrocardiographic tracings or do a venous catheterization. Sydenham would probably be unable to interpret all the liver function tests. Neither Hodgkins nor Bright would be able to do blood morphology and blood chemistry. Yet they were great men and great personalities.

In the time of Hippocrates, Greece was permeated with the spirit of philosophy and ethics, and when the disciples of Hippocrates recited the oath, what an inspiration it must have been in guiding them in their daily tasks in caring for the sick. Yet to us the Hippocratic Oath is likely to be merely a remnant of a curiosity from the Old World. This is true in spite of the fact that we have an example, in the physicians of Germany under the Nazi regime, of how modern medicine, in spite of all of its advancements, when applied without ethics and moral inhibitions can be turned on mankind cruelly and thus increase misery. Modern scientific medicine in Germany had developed to the highest degree, yet the German physicians stooped to the lowest level in human history. They used their so-called scientific research on human beings and treated them worse than rats. Would a disciple of Aesculapius in ancient times, one who recited that oath, ever stoop to such a low level? I believe not. What was the cause of it, then? It seems, to borrow a phrase from Dr. Trueblood, that the Germans developed a "power medicine" without any moral or ethical inhibitions.

What we need is not a modernization of the old Hippocratic Oath but rather a realization that the physician, in addition to his scientific training, has a need for prayer. Once he realizes that need, he will find the right prayer to express his devotion.

At present we are mostly concentrating on the tools of the physician, the products of science, rather than on the person who is to handle these tools. This tendency is universal; science has penetrated the very secrets of the atom, and we can now unleash forces sufficient to destroy the human race on this planet, while man himself has made very little progress in improving his character or raising his moral and ethical values. In medicine, too, we are constantly inculcating in the student the "scientific imperative" rather than the "moral and ethical imperative." Even in the selection of students for medical schools, the humanities, the classics, the cultural background, all are overlooked, and the emphasis is placed on scientific studies. The student who has taken more scientific courses, even though his training may be one-sided, has a better chance of entering a medical school than one with a broader undergraduate education. Then, in the medical schools, constant emphasis is put on research. Encouragement is given to write research papers, while the history and cultural background of medicine are neglected.

In a paper entitled "Medical History as a Prophylactic," the author has enumerated the values and benefits of the study of medical history.[2] The most important factor of all in the building of character in the physician was the instillation in him of a sense of humility.

The thesis of this paper is that prayer too, like medical history, leads to humility and the building of character.

Prayer here does not mean a petition for ordinary wants of our nature and circumstances, or even a request for greater gifts or blessings. Nor does it mean, in the words of Milton, "but prayer for offended Deity to appease," although this too has its value and purpose. As a matter of fact, Dr. Alexis Carell wrote a book in which he showed the good effect of prayer on patients.[3] In this book he says that he has seen cases in which prayer healed human beings both spiritually and physically. Had he followed the outline for prayer as illustrated in this paper, his last years would have been no less noble than his earlier ones.

We are concerned here with the effect that prayer has on the personality of the one who prays—that indescribable emotional experience which molds the character of men. Dr. Richard Cabot describes so beautifully the mood and pause of prayer: "The deep joy of mutual love or parenthood, the decisive victory of the right in national life or in ourselves, brings us that wistful wondering pause, that 'orbed solitude' which is close to prayer."[4]

President Eliot of Harvard stated: "Prayer is the supreme effort of the human intelligence—the effort of finite man to commune with and even speak to the Infinite."[5]

But the clear meaning of prayer was portrayed by a physician of the Middle Ages, namely, Maimonides, who was a philosopher and theologian as well as a physician, and these three faculties complemented and supplemented each other. According to Maimonides, sincere prayer leads to true humility.[6] It is in prayer that a person is supposed to reflect upon the status of the human being in the universe; meditating upon God in the grandeur of His creation leads one to realize the place he occupies therein. For if a person finds himself in the real mood and pause of prayer he feels like exclaiming, in the words of the psalmist: "When I behold Thy heavens, the work of Thy fingers . . . what is man, that Thou art mindful of him?" (Psalm 8:4–5).

It is of extreme interest that the Hebrew word "to pray," *hitpalel*, is a reflexive verb signifying, at least in one sense, self-examination. It is prayer in this sense that gives a meaning to the old maxim, "He who rises from prayer a better man, his prayer is answered."[7] When a physician devotedly prays in solitude, he not only communes with God, he communes with the great spirits of medicine of all ages, and as Professor Edman says: "The ultimate society of the mind, when the spirit listeth, is a soliloquy and that isolated heaven is crowded with friends in the form of congenial themes."[8]

If the prayer impulse is present in the physician, he needs no special place of worship. Isn't the consultation room a sanctuary in itself! If in the examining room a patient reveals his body, it is in the consultation room that he reveals his soul and heart. Nor does the physician need any special stereotyped form of prayer. Here is a prayer by Judah Halevi (ca. 1080–1145) in which he reveals the nobility of character and the humility of a true physician.

The Physician's Prayer

My God, heal me and I shall be healed,
Let not Thine anger be kindled against me so
that I be consumed.
My medicines are of Thee, whether good
Or evil, whether strong or weak.
It is Thou who shalt choose, not I;
Of Thy knowledge is the evil and the fair.
Not upon my power of healing I rely;
Only for Thine healing do I watch.[9]

As for most physicians, who may not be either authors or poets, it seems to me that if they possess the prayer impulse, they can find the right prayer in the Book of Psalms, which has been accepted by practically all humanity. In this book of praise, for centuries men in all generations and in all walks of life have found echoes to their feelings and emotions under various stresses and strains. Here the human spirit has found an outlet to rise to greater heights.

In the following paragraphs I shall briefly describe certain physicians and situations in which they have been involved and suggest prayers and psalms which apply.

The physician who strives to follow the ideals of his profession, and becomes discouraged because he is less successful than some of his competitors who may be less idealistic, may find solace in the following passage from Book of Psalms:

Happy is the man that hath not walked in the counsel of the wicked . . .
And he shall be like a tree planted by streams of water,
That bringeth forth its fruit in its season,
And whose leaf doth not wither;
And in whatsoever he doeth shall prosper. (Psalm 1:1–3)

The successful physician who has remained true to his ideals can find verses in this book to express his inner joy.

G. K. Chesterton wrote, "There is no better test of a man's ultimate chivalry and integrity than how he behaves when he is wrong."[10] This statement applies to physicians, especially in their relations to their colleagues. A prominent surgeon, called in as a consultant, disagreed with the physician in charge concerning a diagnosis, but found, upon operating, that the physician had been right, and admitted it. This required courage and revealed the integrity and inner strength of a real man. This surgeon should thank the Lord for his strength of character and might well recall the Fifteenth Psalm, which describes the ideal human character, known as "God's Gentleman":

> Lord, who shall sojourn in Thy tabernacle?
> Who shall dwell upon Thy holy mountain?
>
> He that walketh uprightly, and worketh righteousness,
> And speaketh truth in his heart;
>
> That hath no slander upon his tongue,
> Nor doeth evil to his fellow,
> Nor taketh up a reproach against his neighbor.

On the other hand, the consultant who disagreed with a physician's diagnosis of coronary disease and angina pectoris and was proven wrong when the patient died, but who has never acknowledged his error, should pray for strength to enable him to admit his mistakes and be as ready to do this as he is to point out the errors of others. The consultant who fails to consider the history of a case and then is angry with the physician when he comes up with an incorrect diagnosis likewise needs prayer for guidance and for the "bigness" to say, "I did not take time to get the whole picture and I was wrong."

Consultation is a sacred duty, and the great physician understands it as such. There are three persons concerned: the patient, who is most important; the physician in charge; and the consultant. The consultant needs prayer to ask for guidance so that he will not be overwhelmed by his own success and importance, so that he will walk humbly before his colleagues and patients.

Unfortunately, consultation and confiscation sometimes become synonymous, particularly when the patient is rich and prominent. The physician in charge is pushed aside. To such a consultant the Fifty-first Psalm, the psalm of penitence, is particularly appropriate.

It would be well for some physicians to memorize a few verses of the Psalms that apply to their particular shortcomings. For the megalo-physician, who strolls about with empty pride, giving the impression that he symbolizes, like the statue of Minerva, all the arts, sciences, and victory, or like a prancing horse on parade, a good prescription might be a daily recitation of these two verses:

Be ye not as the horse, or as the mule, which have no understanding;
Whose mouth must be held in with bit and bridle,
That they come not near unto thee. (Psalm 32:9)

Let not the foot of pride overtake me,
And let not the hand of the wicked drive me away. (Psalm 36: 12)

On the other hand, genuine pride and joy should fill the heart of the physician who is always ready to give a helping hand to anyone who seeks his aid or his counsel. He is concerned neither with the stratum of society to which people belong nor with their ability to remunerate him for his services. He has no fixed fee and is concerned with the poor as well as with the wealthy. Such a physician can proudly say, "Happy is he who considereth the poor" (Psalm 41: 2). The psalmist did not say, "Blessed is he who giveth to the poor," but rather he refers to the man who considers how the meritorious act can best be carried out. In the original text, *dal*, translated as "poor," signified "feeble," not necessarily a poor man. It applies to one enfeebled in health. This verse could well be applied to physicians caring for their fellow physicians as patients. Physicians often receive very poor treatment at the hands of their colleagues. A physician tells the story of how he once suffered an infected finger. When the infection began to spread along the line of the lymphatics, in desperation he phoned a surgeon in the evening, only to be told,

"You know what to do as well as I do. I shall see you in the morning." This surgeon would do well to repeat daily the verse quoted above. Another who would profit by keeping this verse in mind is the physician who told a schoolteacher, when the teacher asked for his services for a member of his family, "You know I am a specialist; you are a teacher and I don't think you will be able to pay my fee." Yes, we do need prayer.

Just as the surgeon scrubs his hands for seven minutes prior to an operation to guard against infection, and just as he places his surgical gown over his clothing to prevent any possible infection, so should we of the medical profession spend at least one minute in prayer and devotion in order to cleanse our souls before coming to the patient. Medicine is as sacred a calling as theology, and prayer is, as we explained, a kind of spiritual aseptic technique.

In a lecture delivered before the Royal Society in April 1920, Rudyard Kipling stated that "about 1600 years ago when Rome was mistress of the world . . . the story goes that Rome allowed all those people one night in the year on which they could say aloud exactly what they thought of Rome, without fear of the consequences."[11] It seems to me that we too might profit by simulating this; instead of glorifying ourselves constantly in mutual admiration, we ought to examine ourselves and see if we are what we think we are and see how others find us. Let us have an annual spiritual examination just as we advise our patients to have annual physical check-ups. By searching our inner selves we shall be able to serve others better. So let us pray!

A good prayer which expresses the ideals set forth in this paper is contained in the so-called Oath and Prayer of Maimonides, which was probably written in a later period by the physician and philosopher Marcus Herz (1747–1803). Whoever wrote it expressed well the ideals of medicine and the functions of the physician. It is a worthwhile prayer, and every physician and student of medicine should be acquainted with it. This prayer is merely a compilation of biblical quotations, most of which are found in the Psalms.

The Oath and Prayer of Maimonides

Thy Eternal Providence has appointed me to watch over the

life and health of Thy creatures. May the love for my art actuate me at all times; may neither avarice, nor miserliness, not the thirst for glory, nor for a great reputation engage my mind; for the enemies of Truth and Philanthropy could easily deceive me and make me forgetful of my lofty aim of doing good to Thy children. May I never see in the patient anything but a fellow creature in pain.

Grant me strength, time, and opportunity always to correct what I have acquired, always to extend its domain; for knowledge is immense and the spirit of man can extend infinitely to enrich itself daily with new requirements. Today he can discover his errors of yesterday and tomorrow he may obtain a new light on what he thinks himself sure of today.

O God, Thou hast appointed me to watch over the life and death of
  Thy creatures; here I am ready for my vocation.
And now I turn unto my calling:
O stand by me, my God, in this truly important task;
Grant me success! For—
Without Thy loving counsel and support,
Man can avail but naught.
Inspire me with true love for this my art
And for Thy creatures, O, grant—
That neither greed for gain, nor thirst for fame, nor vain ambition,
May interfere with my activity.
For these I know are enemies of Truth and Love of men,
And might beguile one in profession,
From furthering the welfare of Thy creatures.
O strenghten me.
Grant energy unto body and the soul
That I might e'er unhindered ready be
To mitigate the woes,
Sustain and help.
The rich and poor, the good and bad, enemy and friend.
O let me e'er behold in the afflicted and suffering
Only the human being.

NOTES

1. D. Elton Trueblood, *The Predicament of Modern Man* (New York: Harper & Brothers, 1944), p. 31.

2. H. A. Savitz, "Medical History as a Prophylactic," *Diplomate*, November 1943. Included in this collection, see p. 139.

3. Alexis Carell, *Prayer* (Morehouse-Gorham Co., 1948).

4. Richard C. Cabot, *What Men Live By* (Boston: Houghton Mifflin).

5. "The Two Hundred and Fiftieth Anniversary of the Settlement of the Jews in the United States," an address delivered in Boston, 1906.

6. "*Mishneh Torah,* Book I, 2:2: "It is mandatory to love and fear God. But how may one learn to love and fear Him? When man will reflect concerning His works and His great and wonderful creatures and will behold through them His wonderful, matchless, and infinite wisdom, he will spontaneously be filled with love, praise, and exultation, and become possessed with a great longing to know the great name, even as David said, 'My soul thirsts for God, for the living God' [Psalm 42:2]. And when he will think of all these matters he will be taken aback in a moment and will be stricken with awe, and will realize that he is an infinitesimal creature, humble and dark, standing with an insignificant and slight knowledge in the presence of the All-Wise."

7. George Meredith, *The Ordeal of Richard Feverel.*

8. Irwin Edman, *Philosopher's Holiday* (New York; Viking Press, 1938).

9. *Selected Poems of Jehudah Halevi* (Philadelphia: Jewish Publication Society, 1928), p. 113.

10. G. K. Chesterton, *The Common Man* (New York: Sheed & Ward).

11. Rudyard Kipling, *Book of Words* (New York: Doubleday, Doran, 1928).

The Other Self: Better or Worse

The human face consists of two asymmetrical halves, and if we were to take a mirror-picture of each half, we should produce two faces of two distinctly different personalities. In the mental life of individuals, too, there are various personalities, such as the "several selves" described by William James. It appears, however, that in each person as we know him there are at least two distinct personalities; one which is apparent to everyone; the other, which, though concealed, is the really active force behind the individual's actions.

Sir James Barrie (1860–1937), Scottish novelist, short story writer, and playwright, in an address delivered at St. Andrew's University on May 3, 1922, described his inner self and gave it the name of Mc'Connochie. "Mc'Connochie is the name I gave to the true half of myself, the writing half. We are complement and supplement. I am the half that is dour and practical and canny; he is the fanciful half!" The great physician Sir William Osler (1849–1919) describes his other half as unruly and worse, and called him Egerton Y. Davis, who wrote and did things of which his sane self would not approve.

These true selves of our personality reveal themselves on various occasions when so to speak, they come out of their hiding places. It is then only that one is able to catch a glimpse of them.

Read before the "Amalgamated," Ḥanukkah, 1951. First published in *Jewish Forum*, February 1952.

The Talmud has a very fine expression which tells us that you can learn about the real qualities of the inner self of a man: *bekhiso, bekhoso, u-vekha'aso,* "by his pocketbook, by his cup, and by his anger." In other words, we can judge a person's true self by his generosity, by what he says when intoxicated and free of inhibition, and by the manner of his actions when he is emotional and angry. The real self is suppressed; it is kept in chains, confined; but on these occasions it is free from its lord and master and appears in its true form.

The physician has the opportunity, at times, of viewing the inner self of his patients and their families through their actions during an illness. On such occasions the guards are down, and the inner self comes to the surface. At other times little coincidences will reveal the true self of a person. The following example will illustrate: Some years ago I was called to see a poor, modest Jew who lived in one of our poorest neighborhoods, in a two-room apartment, the living room of which was used as a bedroom at night. He was lying on the couch in the poorly furnished room where poverty stared at you from every corner. After examining him, I assured him that there was nothing seriously wrong with him. I was anxious to find out what type of man he was, for I could see that, in spite of his shabby appearance, there was a penetrating sparkle in his eye. Above the couch there hung on the wall a portrait of great rabbis, the central figure of which was Maimonides. I pointed to this picture wondering if he knew who he was and said, "Who is this man? Is he a politician?" Here the man burst into a stream of speech; even his voice took on a new tone as though another person were talking. "Oh, no, Doctor," he replied resentfully, "he was a great philosopher and a great physician. Had he been alive today he would have been a professor at a university." His face lit up. The sick man vanished and a changed person ran to the other side of the room, where there was a shabby bookcase covered with a dusty curtain. Pulling aside the curtain, he took out various writings of Maimonides. He began to reveal their contents, and as he did so, his inner self, his real personality, was also revealed—one of which very few people were aware.

The following episode, on the other hand, reveals a different kind of personality which is totally opposite from the one previously described. A woman came to me weeping to ask about her mother's condition. Her illness was due to a cerebro-vascular accident. She was living by herself on a substantial sum of money assigned to her on separation from her husband.

Bursting into tears, she cried, "My poor mother! How she must be suffering!"

I assured the woman that her mother was not suffering any physical pain, and she questioned, "How long will it last? There isn't much money left. Perhaps she should go into a public institution in a ward."

I told the daughter that I had promised never to send her mother to a public institution. To the daughter's great relief, her mother died shortly thereafter, and there was a sufficient amount of money left for her. It was evident that while one part of her shed tears for her mother's condition, the other part shed tears for her mother's estate, which was rapidly diminishing as a result of private nursing. Each teardrop seemed to be composed of two droplets.

In the following paragraphs I wish to describe various types of selves buried beneath the surface of individuals. Borrowing the nomenclature of Sir James Barrie, I should like to describe several types of inner selves. The one most easily identified I like to call by the name of "McKilas" (from the Hebrew, for miser). Although he is a gentleman on the surface, his following the customs and manners of his age is merely a thin veneer, for the real person is selfish, unconcerned with any one but himself. The motives of selfishness color whatever he does. Friends are used merely for furthering his own gains. He acts as if he were the center of the universe and the rest of the world was merely his backyard.

There is still another "inner self" that operates maliciously within some people. I like to call this type of inner person "McIvy." He is the vulgar social-climber. He is crude, antisocial, and has a definite inferiority complex. He steps over most people; being insensitive, he cares little for other people's feelings. He acts like a master to most people he knows; in reality, however, he is a slave. Being obedient, he bows with servility to others whom he considers to be of the highest strata. Although to certain people he is unpolished, he can be very smooth, like the green leaves of the ivy plant, with those into whose society he would like to enter. Like the ivy plant, he clings to them, and by them he tries to reach what he considers a higher level. He is never himself. He always feels insecure. Like the ivy plant, again, he grows in all climates and in all lands. Especially is this true of the nouveau-riche, or those who have joined a certain profession with no cultural background in past generations. Professor Harry A. Wolfson artistically describes this type, which flourished in Alexandria during the time of Philo. One could do no better than to quote him:

Another motive of apostasy discussed by Philo is that which may be described as the vulgar delusion of social ambition. Wealth in the Alexandrian Jewish community was derived from the non-Jewish environment through contacts with heathens. Such contacts with heathens thus became financial assets, and financial assets naturally became marks of a delusive social distinction, and the delusion of social distinction, in turn, led to snobbishness, obsequiousness, self-effacement, aping, simulation, pretense, and ultimately to a begging for permission to join whatever one had to join in order to become a heathen.

There is another self in some people which I call "McYohir" (which comes from the root of the Hebrew word *yahir*, "boastful") or what is known in the vernacular as a snob. A snob is defined as a person who admires, imitates, or cultivates those of social rank, wealth, etc., with an air of condescension or overbearingness toward others. This type of personality involves the habit of arrogating deference to oneself. This self does not reveal merely pride, for it involves the element of conceit; one imagines himself as possessing that which is not his. There is also an element of haughtiness, for this person breathes a superior atmosphere to other people. He also possesses an element of vanity, for he wants more to be admired than approved; and in such a way it is a form of self-conceit which attempts to fool others and appear in such light as he is not. "He who is proud has a certain blemish" (Megilah 29).

This is well portrayed by the eloquent preacher Jacob ben Wolf Kranz (1741–1804), known as the "Dubner Maggid." He says that the snob, the *ba'al ga'avah*, not only fools others but, what is even worse, he eventually fools himself. This is further explained in his customary homespun fable:

This is like unto a man who befriended and made welcome to his house a thief whose purpose was to sell him the goods stolen from others. After a while, the man, to his amazement, discovered that the thief was robbing him also of all his possessions. Whereupon the man complained to his neighbors, "Look what he has done to me. I have made him my friend, made my house open to him, and now he robs me." His neighbors replied, "You fool, if he steals from others, he will not spare you." And so the man of conceit may fool others but he is in reality his own victim. He actually believes himself to be what he is not.*

In contrast to this self, there is another which I call "McHalom" (from the Hebrew root *halom*, "dream"). No matter how practical one self tries to be, the other self wanders off and dreams on. This self is detached from reality, seeking his own patterns and imageries. This self may be the reverse of the man and his profession. An example of this type is Theodor Herzl (1840–1904), the founder of modern political Zionism. He was a prominent publicist by profession, but he had another self that was constantly dreaming about a Jewish state. Here is what he says in his *Diaries* about the book he wrote, *The Jewish State:*

It has the appearance of a mighty dream; but for days and weeks it has been permeating my whole being, down even into the region of subconsciousness; has accompanied me everywhere, hovered above my ordinary conversations, glanced over my shoulder into the absurdly trivial occupations of the journalist, disturbed and intoxicated me.

This dreaming self is immortalized, for dreams are contagious, and when the person dies, his dream is usually carried on. So when, in his colossal effort in behalf of his dream, Herzl broke his body and died in the prime of life, his dream was carried on by others, among whom was Dr. Chaim Weizmann, a president of Israel, who by profession was a cold, logical scientist, and who, when he entered his laboratory, took nothing for granted except the facts as revealed in the experiments in the laboratory. On the other hand, he possessed another self whose dream was a homeland for the Jewish people. In spite of all the

*See above, p. 67, for a biographical study of the Dubner Maggid.

obstacles and handicaps and hardships, he never abandoned that dream, and lived long enough to see it realized. In other words, there were two Weizmanns: one, the chemist, who deals with formulae and facts and takes nothing for granted unless it is proven; the other, the dreamer, who in spite of the facts holds on to his dream and finds his dream a reality.

On the other hand, there are people whose other selves fuse together and produce a composite personality. For example, Maimonides was a physician, philosopher, and theologian, and the three complemented and supplemented each other. It is difficult to tell where the philosopher ends and the doctor begins or where the doctor ends and the theologian begins. Maimonides belongs to that group of personalities which personify genius; this kind of personality revealing a peculiar glow of its own.

There is still another type of whom the selves are diametrically opposed and yet they fuse together. Such a person was Shalom Rabinovitz (1859–1916), whose pen name was Shalom Aleichem. Shalom Rabinovitz was the pathetic character, the man who suffered in silence. Shalom Aleichem was the one who saw the humorous side no matter how tragic the situation. Whenever Shalom Rabinovitz had tears in his eyes, Shalom Aleichem had a smile on his lips; his genius and humor could make his entire people laugh, even though internally he was a very sad and suffering person, and at the time when he laughed the loudest, he suffered the most. This is well revealed in the epitaph which he wrote for himself. The following is a translation by I.G.:

> Here lies a simple-hearted Jew,
>   Whose Yiddish womenfolk delighted;
> And all the common people, too,
>   Laughed at the stories he indited;
>
> Poked fun at life as but a jest,
>   Laughed up his sleeve at all that mattered;
> When other men were happiest,
>   Alas, his heart was bruised and shattered.
>
> Most often when his audience
>   Applauded and was laughter ridden,

He ailed, which God's Conscience
Alone remarked, He kept it hidden.

This is why the characters of Shalom Aleichem reflect the dual personality of the author himself. They are not merely comic characters that arouse pure laughter but rather comico-tragic figures, characters that invoke laughter in us and at the same time break the hearts of readers so that they are forced to shed tears. It is in such a manner that Shalom Aleichem succeeded in mirroring the Eastern Jews of which he was an integral part.

It seems to me that in nations too we can detect the real personality of a people—the other self—for example, when that nation is involved in a severe conflict such as war. The cruelty practiced by the Nazis during their regime, and particularly during the war, reveals the other self hidden in the German people. One can also understand the personality of a nation's people by its folk literature. Like the dreams of an individual, which reveal the desires of the inner self, so the legends of a people reveal the inner makeup of a nation. There is considerable Jewish folk literature which deals with the Messianic age, and it seems that it permeated the mind of every Jew, and each Jew seems to contain a little Messiah in him. Just as a radioactive luminescence is visible when lights are turned off, so the Jew in his darkest period has that ray of hope which helps him to survive. It is interesting to note that the song developed in the concentration camps was "I Believe in the Coming of the Messiah."

When Freud first started his method of investigations in the field of psychoanalytic psychology, he developed what he called the id, which is that part of the subconscious which strives to fulfill all the innate desires and appetites. Later in life, Freud developed the concept of the superego, which is the conscience that guides and controls the id. The libido represents all the instinctual energies and desires which are derived from the id, the innate actuating or impelling force in living beings. The superego is the psychic apparatus which mediates between id drives and social ideals, and acts as a conscience which may be partly conscious and partly unconscious. If the id, according to Freud, would be the devil, then the superego would be the equivalent of an angel. After further analysis, is that not the equivalent of the Jewish concept which has been preached for the past two thousand years! The *yezer ha-ra,* or "evil inclination," in every man is usually personified in Hebrew literature. Its counter-distinction, the *yezer ha-tov,* "good nature," the inclination to do good, is also personified; and as the rabbis explained the phrase in Genesis 2:7, "and God created man"(*vayizer* in Hebrew is spelled with two *yudim*), the word is so spelled because every man has two instincts—one to do good, and the other to do evil. Noble deeds can be the result of a primary evil inclination, while very terrible acts are often the result of preaching high ideals. A great many people are fooled today by a proposal of universal peace and equality for all races and creeds, though we know what happens in a totalitarian state. Equality is reduced to equal servitude for all, and every individual is a slave to the state. On the other hand, when one gives up certain freedoms, one finds that restriction is often a means of obtaining the highest freedom.

It is evident that the human individual is a complex personality of several selves, each one striving to dominate. On certain occasions, the dominant personality is revealed. Happy is the man who can integrate the undesirable self within him so as to make all of his selves work in harmony toward a common creative goal. This is what is meant by the saying of the rabbis: "thou shalt love the Lord thy God with both the *yezer ha-ra* and the *yezer ha-tov.*" In other words, one should love the Lord with the evil instinct as well as with the good instinct.

Spiritual Rickets

Analogy, according to the rules of logic, is not a proper form to prove an argument, yet it is helpful in visualizing and grasping a complicated thought. It often throws light and makes objects visible that are elusive and easily overlooked.

It is with this idea in mind that the following analogy from the field of medicine is selected to demonstrate the vital importance of Hebrew culture to the continuity of a normal, full Jewish life.

One of the outstanding contributions of modern scientific medicine is found in the understanding of the disease known as rickets, or what the layman calls softening of the bones.

A number of children, particularly those whose ancestors came from parts of the world where sunshine is plentiful, become victims of this dreadful malady when they are born in temperate climates and are robbed of the natural rays of the sun.

Particularly is it true of those children who are deprived of natural mother's milk, and an artificial formula is substituted for it.

Here is a description of this malady in its classical form. The child lies listless, there is cold perspiration around the forehead, the abdomen protrudes, the legs are bowed, the muscles are flabby, the skeleton is deformed, the child cannot stand upright, the framework of the body is soft, the slightest injury produces a fracture which extends further the crippling and deformity.

It seems to me that, turning away from the physical world to the spiritual, we can find a similar disease that I would like to call spiritual rickets.

First published in *Brandeis Avukah Annual,* 1932.

207

Jewish youth born and raised under Palestinian skies and nurtured in the Hebrew tongue grow into complete, normal, fully developed Jews. A Palestinian youth reared in the land of the Bible, in the tongue of the Bible, develops a spiritual skeleton that keeps him upright and erect, facing the world as a man and as a Jew.

A Palestinian child who reads the history of his people in the surrounding numerous tombstones and graves where every stretch of land marks a new chapter in the history of his people, finds in these pages a stimulant to his character and a solid framework to his mental makeup. Thus he can absorb the cultures of other people and never feel inferior to them.

On the other hand, when Jewish children are born on foreign soil, and are brought up among foreign tongues and cultures, they develop a spiritual malady when they grow up that one may call, by analogy, spiritual rickets.

When in a group of other nationalities, the young Jew will discuss with enthusiasm and vigor any vital problem concerning human endeavors, but as soon as the conversation veers around to his own people and to his own culture, we find him acquiring signs and symptoms of this disease. His posture stoops, his face flushes, a cold sweat covers his brow; he appears to have lost his mental courage, his spirit wilts, he is subject to injury at the slightest reference to his people. This is a frequent spectacle to be observed among our college students. They may excel in the various arts and sciences, may be able to discuss all matters with diligence and vehemence, yet they lack the courage and manhood to withstand or even discuss intelligently any problem that concerns the Jewish race.

This is often true of those of the Jewish race who have attained high levels in some academic field and occupy prominent positions in the universities.

This analogy can be further extended in its logical sequence, and the same treatment can be applied to the mental field as well as to the physical. Modern medicine has discovered that it can make up for the deficiency of the healthful rays of the sun through the substitution of cod liver oil. God and Nature have been kind, and as in the words of the homely old adages, there is a remedy for each ailment. It appears that the rays of the sun are somehow stored in seaweed, and when the cod feed upon this, the sun's rays are preserved in their oils.

Those children who fall victims to rickets, when fed with these oils, are restored to normal health and development. Their perspiration disappears, their skeleton hardens, their muscles grow firm, they are able to stand upright, they gain vigor, they become playful and develop into normal adults.

The same remedy should be applied to Jewish youth who, by the accident of birth, are not privileged to live in Palestine.

Hebrew literature, which found its origin and developed under Palestinian skies and sunshine, is preserved in books, beginning with the ancient literature of the Bible, with the epic of Moses, and continuing up to the lyrics and epics of Ḥayyim Naḥman Bialik. Hand in hand with the general culture must come a foundation of culture in the Hebrew tongue. Only through such a medium shall we develop normal healthy Jews who will never suffer from spiritual rickets.

In any group, wherever they may find themselves, they will stand upright as proud men and Jews, and in all discussions the Jew will take and give, appreciating the views of others and giving back something of his own in exchange. It is only in such a way that we shall attain a mutual understanding and tolerance with ourselves and with the world at large.

The Anatomy of Hebrew Words

A number of Jews have raised the question, "Why spend so many of the child's years in the study of Hebrew, when the essentials of Judaism can be taught in English?" I shall endeavor to answer this question by a brief study of the anatomy of Hebrew words.

A word, by definition, is an articulate sound or combination of sounds expressing an idea. However, this is as inadequate as the dictionary's definition of blood—the fluid which circulates in the arteries and veins of an animal. Volumes have been written on this fluid. Who has not heard of the fractionization of blood during the last war and the miracles performed with these fractions? From the study of a single drop of blood, a physician can tell whether a person is ill or not and in some cases can prognosticate the outcome.

Words, too, are organic and vital; they grow and, in the process of evolution, take on new meanings. The very soul of a people is to be sought in the meaning of the words it develops. The words of a language carry within them the trophies of glorious victories of the past. But more important, like the serum in the blood, which contains antibodies to counteract diseases, so words contain the armor that portects people. Words grow and develop, and at times they degenerate and lose their inner vital forces. That is why, in a sense, it is impossible to translate from one language into another. At best, a translation is merely like a photograph in black and white of a living, fragrant rose. Only a rare genius can recreate from one language into

First published in *Jewish Forum,* April 1947.

another. Even then it is only a reproduction in color photography of the real thing. They are seldom the same.

As an illustration, a word we all know; namely, "gentleman." Originally it meant a person belonging to the nobility. Then, in the process of evolution, it took on so many attributes that it applied to any individual with all the visible and invisible yet noble characteristics who might be distinguished and pointed out, "Here is a perfect gentleman." A whole monograph could be written on what constitutes a gentleman. But no one word in any language will convey the same group of characteristics designated by the word "gentleman." To mention a few of these attributes, a gentleman is a person well-bred or educated, raised above the common herd, above the vulgar. He is chivalrous, kind—his every deed and the very words he utters carry such atmosphere with them.

The word "gentleman," with its multiple connotations of nobility, also illustrates how a word can degenerate and be left an empty shell, even harboring decayed matter. This process was revealed before our very eyes in the 1930s and 1940s. A Fascist or a Nazi is the antithesis of a gentleman. He is crude, vulgar, false, and brutal. When he has a desire, he murders and appropriates—with no finesse in so doing. A British gentleman, on the other hand, would never dare do things in so crude a manner. If he desires oil for the Royal Navy, he creates incidents by which he divides the population of a country against one another and comes in as protector. As a chivalrous, kind man, he cannot see injustice done, so he partitions the country—a remnant for one, a village for the other—and keeps the rest for himself. That is Nazi cruelty in the empty shell of a gentleman.

To describe such evil under the cover of piety, we have an expression in Hebrew—*huzpah*—which cannot be translated into any other language. It means more than "audacity," "shamelessness," "insolence," or even "impudence." It is all these terms imply, plus. A New York columnist defined *huzpah* with the illustration of a person who, in cold blood, murdered his father and mother, and pleads for the mercy of the court because he is now an orphan. As a matter of fact, the English language, unable to translate *huzpah*, has accepted it as it is.

Or take the simple Hebrew word *sefer*, which literally means "book." To the student of Hebrew literature, it has a much more profound meaning and leads to a number of allusions and associations which are lost in translation. When Jews in their long journey, due to various circumstances, adopted a new language and wanted to express the full meaning of a word, they used the original word mixed in the sentences of their native tongue. For example, if a person wrote a book for entertainment, or as a source of information, he was designated as the author of a "book," *buch* or *buechel*. But if he wrote a book that was destined to shape the course of a people or mold their character, they called him the *mehaber*, "author," of a *sefer*.

A book was to be read or even re-read; but a *sefer* was to be studied. The entire approach to a *sefer* was different. It was handled with care and reverence. If it fell to the ground, it was lifted and kissed. When it became shabby and torn beyond repair, it was buried among its devoted readers. The very *mezuzah* that marks the entrance of a Jewish home is merely a piece of parchment upon which is inscribed a famous chapter from the *sefer*, the Torah, that is respected by all observant Jews. The house of the author of a *sefer* is regarded as a shrine today by Jews in Palestine. The *sefer* represents the symbolic paper bridge found in Jewish lore which is included in cradle lullabies—the Jews will march on a paper bridge and arrive at their promised land, while the heathens will march on an iron bridge, which will eventually cave in, leaving those depending on it to drown. If one is to find a short formula to portray the secret of Jewish survival, one could say, "The Jews preserved the *sefer*, and the *sefer* in turn preserved them."

No single word in any language portrays the Jew's sorrow with all its ramifications during his entire two thousand years of wandering as does the Hebrew word *galut*. The words "exile" and "diaspora" do not give an inkling of the entire tragic picture. By merely using the untranslated word *galut* as the prefix—for example, "*galut* psychology"—one can fathom the deep-seated evil produced in a people that is homeless, a homelessness which tears apart the very pattern of its personality. By the one term "*galut* psychology," we understand the process of some *galut* Jews, their lack of dignity and self-respect. It is the *galut* which leads to self-abasement, a tendency to mimicry and even self-hatred. This is well portrayed in the galaxy of Jews portrayed in the book *Germany's Step-Children*—which can be summarized in one word, *galut*. No wonder the rabbis of old warned their disciples of the punishment for misconduct expressed in the words, "Ye may be condemned to *galut* [exile]"—for the word *galut* expresses a chain reaction as in atomic fission—once it starts, one reaction after another leads to the destruction of the soul of the exiled. No punishment can compare in its severity.

Take the word *Shekhinah*, which in translation at best means "Divine Presence" or "holy inspiration"—yet the translation is equally inadequate. It would require a gifted poet to describe in verse, or a gifted artist to paint with brush, a man who in Hebrew is described by the words, "The *Shekhinah* hovers over him." Such a person is more than a saint with a halo around his head, or a gifted scholar. It is all-inclusive. It would take several medical essays written by experts in medicine as well as the pen to convey the Hebrew concept that "the *Shekhinah* hovers over the headside of the sick man's bed." Who knows how much this adage inspired the great rabbi-physicians in the Middle Ages so that their services were sought by popes and kings and lay people alike. How many sociological treatises could be written about the Jews in the diaspora expressing the talmudic thought that "Whithersoever they were exiled, the *Shekhinah* went with them" (*Bava Batra* 25a)?

There was an ancient Hebrew sage and martyr of the second century, Hananiah ben Teradyon, an expert in uttering eternal truths briefly and beautifully, whose dying words were, "The Parchment is being burned, but its characters keep flying in the atmosphere, for their message cannot be destroyed." When this wise man wanted to express the benefits that come from intellectual intercourse, from literary clubs where time is devoted to the interchange of ideas, he expressed all the rewards—joy, utility, and atmosphere created by this one Hebrew word. He said, "But if two sit together and interchange words of Torah, the *Skekhinah* abides between them."

That brings me to the next word—"Torah." Originally, *torah* meant "instruction" or "law"—from the verb *yoreh*, "to teach." It was applied at first to the Law of Moses—the Pentateuch. Then it included all the Jewish books of law, and later it signified learning in general. Much has been written on the meaning of Torah in Jewish life—much more could be written to show to what heights Torah, the concept of scholarship, has been developed. Torah became the standard of measurement. Man was respected and graded according to his knowledge of the Torah. Premiums were placed on scholarship. The scholar was held in higher esteem than the high priest. Even the Almighty looked into the Torah and then created the universe. In other words, the Torah came before the universe, and the universe exists for the sake of the Torah. This concept has a great deal of truth and realism—it is more than mere poetry in this atomic age into which we have just been hurled.

Then came the intellectual joy of scholarship and study for its own sake, as expressed by the term *Torah lishmah*, "learning for its own sake." This is the greatest intellectual joy in life, and it explains why so many Jews were physicians during the so-called Dark Ages. For to the Jew, education meant knowing everything that was to be known; and medicine was an important branch of general knowledge. So they were physicians and rabbis as well.

Jewish law emphasizes the study of Torah above all the other commandments. All the rules of etiquette and all the social customs would leave man crude and unpolished if he did not have the luster of education. As expressed in the *Sayings of the Fathers*, "Where there is no Torah, there are no manners." When we abandoned Hebrew, the word Torah shed its multitude of meanings and beautiful concepts, and was left like the trunk of a tree without its foliage. To some American Jews, Torah is an object of curiosity—the scroll of parchment having significance only for preservation in a museum.

Finally, the Hebrew word *ẓedakah* is not translatable either by "charity" or by "philanthropy." As its root designates, it stands for "purity, righteousness, liberality, almsgiving," but a perusal of Jewish literature, including belles-lettres, will reveal to what heights the concept of *ẓedakah* developed—that it is impossible to translate it without writing a book about it; even then its full meaning would not be adequatedly treated. *Ẓedakah* is a deed of love that involves not only the material value but also the personality of the donor himself, as well as his attitude toward the recipient. According to Maimonides, there are several grades of charity including such significance. According to the full developed Hebrew term, *zedakah* does more for the donor than for the recipient. *Zedakah* is not given to save one's soul or to lead one to heaven after death. It raises the *ba'al zedakah*, "benefactor," to a realm higher than heaven during his life, as is so beautifully expressed in Peretz's story "If Not Higher." *Zedakah* defies death and makes man immortal. The expression *Zedakah tazil mimavet*, "*Zedakah* rescues from death," chanted at Jewish funerals, is symbolic. In order to be appreciated, such meaning has to be read in the orginal Hebrew.

In conclusion, it must be noted that the number of such Hebrew words that could be studied is indefinite. Throughout the ages, simple words have acquired meanings which cannot be translated by a single word, or even by sentences, into another language. The translation of a large number of Hebrew words is merely the capsule that contains the vitamin for the very Jewish soul and spirit. The legacy of Israel is often contained in one Hebrew word. If we really wish to survive and continue the thread of Hebraic culture, we must drink from the fountain of the Hebrew language in its original form or we are destined to become dehydrated Jews. This is the highest meaning of Zionism and the rebirth of the Jew in Palestine. In the words of Hananiah, the Jew and his books may be burned but the letters soar upward. We must capture these words and make them part of our mental economy. If we preserve these words in their original meaning they will preserve us to carry on and light the torch in a darkened confused world.

The following stanza from an English poem by Adelaide Anne Procter, who wrote about one hundred years ago, conveys some of our meaning:

> Words are mighty, words are living:
>   Serpents with their venomous stings,
> Or bright angels, crowding round us,
>   With heaven's light upon their wings:
> Every word has its own spirit,
>   True or false, that never dies;
> Every word man's lips have uttered
>   Echoes in God's skies.

Hebraic Word Fission

We have recently been initiated into the Atomic age. Little by little science has succeeded in peeling off nature's secrets, one layer after the other. It finally has succeeded in pentrating the secrets of the very structure of the atom. The theoretically derived concept of atomic structure is that the atom is composed of a positively charged nucleus surrounded and electrically neutralized by negatively charged electrons, revolving in orbits at varying distances from the nucleus, the constitution of the nucleus and the arrangement of the electrons differing with the different chemical elements. When we succeed in knocking out one electron, a new substance is formed and at the same time releases a tremendous amount of energy.

On Ḥanukkah, the Feast of Dedication commemorating the victory of the Maccabees, there is an old Jewish custom to play with tops on which are inscribed four letters—*nun, gimmel, hey,* and *shin,* signifying *Nes gadol hayah sham,* meaning "a great miracle occurred there." The very letters in the word *Maccabee* mean *Mi khamokhah ba'elim Adonai,* "Who is like Thee among the gods?" So in the spirit of Ḥanukkah and, with atomic fission in our mind, as an intellectual exercise, let us apply the same method to Hebrew words. Let us play the game by knocking out one letter of a Hebrew word, just as a physicist would remove an electron in atomic fission, and see what happens.

Take the Hebrew word *rosh,* "head," which is spelled *resh, alef,*

Read before the "Amalgamated," Ḥanukkah 1949. First published in *Jewish Forum,* January 1950.

shin. If we knock out the *alef* and reverse the other two letters, we have the word *shor,* "ox." The letter *alef* itself means "to learn." If you cast out learning from the head, what is left is *shor,* "ox." If you leave the two letters in the same order, you have the word *rash,* "poor man"—and one is poor indeed without the possession of knowledge or learning. As Benjamin Franklin said, "I save my money in my head."

Take the word *rofe,* "doctor," which is spelled *resh, fe, alef.* If you take out the *alef,* you are left with the letters *fe, resh,* which means "bull." A doctor who does not continue to study may become as dangerous as a fighting bull. The same can be applied to the word *adam,* "man"—spelled *alef, dalet, mem.* If you remove the *alef,* "learning," you are left with the word *dam,* "blood." Man can be very dangerous and may cause a great deal of bloodshed once knowledge and learning is eliminated.

Ish, "man," is spelled *alef, yod, shin; ishah,* "woman," *alef, shin, hey.* If you remove the *yod* from *ish* and the *hey* from *ishah,* which two letters spell *yah,* "God," you are left in each case with the word *esh,* "fire." One need not strain his imagination to see the moral lesson in that—when the divine spark is removed from the human species, it is a source of danger. When man utilizes the divine spark, he produces great inventions, makes great discoveries in science, learns how to harness the forces of nature, and may succeed in creating great works of art, music, and literature. On the other hand, when the divine spark is removed from man, he may become one of the most dangerous sources of destruction.

This brings me to a beautiful Midrash about the creation of man. It is said that when God created man, he mated an angel with a horse and the product was man. From one point of view, man's creative powers make him almost angelic in ability; on the other hand, man's inhumanity to man, and the various cruelties he has invented, reveal the beast in him.

The letter *yod* in Hebrew symbolized "hand." Take the word *ashir,* "rich," which is spelled *ayin, shin, yod, resh:* remove the letter *yod,* you are left with the word *rasha,* spelled *resh, shin, ayin,* which means "evil" or "wicked." In other words, if you remove the helping hand from the rich, he is, indeed, a wicked man.

The next Hebrew radical lends itself to mental gymnastics.

The Hebrew word *laham,* "to fight," originally meant "to devour"; in other words, in battle, one is supposed to devour and destroy the enemy. That is why we get the Hebrew noun *lehem,* "bread," which comes from the same origin. When the word is broken up, the letters of the same root, reversed or read backwards, spell *mahal,* "to forgive." It is interesting to note how the same Hebrew root when read one way means "to fight"— ready to destroy—yet reversed, means "to forgive"—suggesting that one be ready to forgive and forget. The same letters inverted spell *halam,* which means "to dream." Here, with a little stretch of the imagination, one can, in this root, visualize the modern theories of the dream; for according to Freudian psychology, the dream is the result of a suppressed wish struggling to break through the censor and come into the consciousness of the sleeping person, after it has been modified and distorted and appears innocuous, so as not to disturb the sleeper.

The Hebrew word *yad,* "hand," in addition to a helping hand, may also symbolize "taking, grabbing." In reverse the letters spell *dai,* "sufficient." The same is true of the Hebrew word *zahav,* "gold," which comes from the root "to glitter"— something that is attractive, something one wishes to accumulate and hoard. In reverse, the letters spell *hazah,* "to despise."

A very fine example of word-splitting is the very name *Israel.* It may be divided into two words, *yashar el,* "straight with the Lord." If the Jewish republic will live up to its name, we trust it will be a model state for the rest of the world.

A classical example of word-splitting is found in the book of Jewish mysticism—the Zohar. The word *Elohim,* "God," the Zohar divides into two words, *mah eileh,* "what are these?" Many a discovery has been made when man, focusing his mind, began to ask, "What is this? Why is it so?" Such was the result of a question preceding the discovery of the law of gravitation, or the accidental observation of the failure of bacteria to grow on a culture on which there were molds, thus leading to the discovery by Dr. Fleming of the miracle drug—penicillin.

Even splitting up of the very letters of Hebrew words is fascinating. A Jewish physician of the fifteenth century, Abraham de Balmes (1440–1523), who wrote the first Hebrew grammar, entitled *Mikneh Avram,* in describing the letters of the

Hebrew alphabet says that the final letter, *tav,* is made up of two components, *nun* and *resh,* which spell "candle." The deeply moral significance of this we discover when we consider that the final result of all learning is to shed light on some dark corner so as to extend our field of knowledge. The Hebrew language itself offers such field, in which we can find great moral lessons and mental enjoyment as we study word roots and even the component letters.

This method of word-splitting is not new in Hebrew literature. Jewish scholars in every generation, for thousands of years, applied it in their study of Scripture. It is said in the Talmud (*Kiddushin* 30a). "They were called scribes, for they recorded or counted all the letters of the Torah." Every word and letter had a multitude of meanings. It is no wonder, then, that they decreed that if a scroll of the Torah had some words obliterated, it was unfit for reading at services. Dr. Abraham de Balmes, in his grammar, wrote: "Our ancestors studied even the combination or arrangement of letters that made up words." This is known in Hebrew as *zirufei otiyot.* For example, the word *oneg,* "pleasure," reversed, spells *nega,* "plague."

There are in the Bible fifteen hundred words or word forms which occur only once. They are called *hapax legomena.* Our sages explained some of these words by breaking them up into their component parts. For example, the word *avrekh,* a word cried out by the heralds before Joseph's chariot (Genesis 41:43), the meaning of which is obscure, was homiletically explained by the rabbis of the Talmud as being composed of two words, *av* and *rekh,* meaning "father" and "tender"; in other words, "father in wisdom, tender in years." Another word in this category, *talpiot* (Canticles 1:1): "Thy neck is like the Tower of David built with turrets." Now the etymology of this word is obscure, and again the rabbis explained it by breaking it up into two words, *tal* and *piot,* "a hill to which everybody turns."

A study of Hebrew words as well as Hebrew literature reveals the Hebrew language as the only key to our Scriptures. The very structure of each word is full of meaning. Even the arrangement of the letters within a word is frequently significant. To read the Bible in a translation into any other language is like observing an intricate tapestry from the wrong side. We may get a faint outline of the figures in the design; however, we fail to appreciate the harmony of the fusion of colors and the intricacy of the design. Not only do we find courage and comfort in our literature, but the very words of the Hebrew language also afford food for the mind and play for the imagination. At times we must exclaim that Hebrew is indeed *lashon hakodesh,* a "holy language" fit for priests and prophets, in which they conversed with God and delivered the messages to man. There still emanates a radiant, glowing energy from the Hebrew words of the prophets, appealing to men's hearts, to make this world a peaceful paradise. If mankind is guided by such radiation, instead of being destroyed by that of atomic fission, all will enjoy eternal peace in the world.

Index

Compiled by Robert J. Milch

221